RUTH LEA

O P T I M A

STOP SMOKING

DR PATRICK KINGSLEY

An OPTIMA book

First published in 1992 by
Macdonald Optima, a division of
Macdonald & Co. (Publishers) Ltd

A member of Maxwell Macmillan Publishing Corporation

Macdonald & Co (Publishers) Ltd
165 Great Dover St
London
SE1 4YA

Photoset in Futura by 🅰 Tek Art Ltd,
Addiscombe, Croydon, Surrey
Printed and bound in Great Britain by Cox & Wyman Ltd,
Reading, Berks

Contents

Introduction

Let us get a few facts clear from the start. Firstly, smoking is bad for you. No-one who reads news-papers or watches television or listens to the radio can fail to be aware of that. Secondly, nobody *needs* to smoke; those who are still smoking gener-ally started, either as a teenager or when they were even younger, to be part of a gang, to look grown-up, or to appear sophisticated. Thirdly, smokers who are honest with themselves wish they had never started, and try to ensure that their children do not start. Fourthly, the main reason for not being able to give up is because of the fear of the withdrawal symptoms that will result, although some think smoking actually makes them feel better. Fifthly, there is never a 'right time' for habitual smokers to give up — they say they will do so when they are ready, but they never are. Finally, while most smokers are addicted to nicotine, they do not really understand what an addiction is or how to deal with it, nor do they realize how minimal their addiction often is.

In my practice I see a great many people who

are addicted to many different things – from tobacco to alcohol and coffee – and they nearly always overcome their addictions without too much difficulty. What has helped them is the fact that they have come to understand *why* they are addicted to these substances, what addiction is all about and how it can be overcome. Once they understand all these things, they can go on to deal with their own particular problems.

In this book I will give a variety of explanations that should help you appreciate what you are doing to yourself and will make you think about what smoking is all about. I hope to make you first analyse your thoughts on smoking so that you come to realize that smoking is not necessary to you. I will demonstrate that withdrawal symptoms are not what you think they are and do not need to be feared. If they do occur, I will show you how to deal with them. I will then describe, step by step, three different methods of stopping smoking.

One point cannot be over-emphasized. No method of giving up smoking will have any chance of success if you do not want to give up and have no intention of doing so. If, however, you really have decided to give up, for whatever reason – cost, health, a nagging family member, the fact that all your friends and colleagues have given up, notices everywhere not allowing you to smoke in public places, or just because you have decided it is about time *you* gave up — reading this book should help you once and for all to kick the smoking habit and never to want to start again.

Most importantly: DO NOT STOP SMOKING YET. Read through the whole book first to see what I am getting at and understand the mechanisms I am trying to explain. Then read the book through a second time, making specific notes about what *you* must do to give up smoking. If necessary, go through Chapter 11 again, which summarizes what I have suggested, and then the best of luck to you. Once you have finally given up (after all those previous attempts), you will feel as if a great load has been lifted from you and you will feel happy about your decision.

1
The dangers of smoking

You may feel as if you have heard so much already about the dangers of smoking that you cannot face reading the details again. But they are worth reiterating, and thinking over, to reinforce your intention to give up.

The most publicized effect of smoking is cancer of the lung. There can no longer be any doubt about this association, but it is often argued that because not everyone who smokes gets cancer of the lung the case is not proven. Everyone knows of, or has been told of, someone who lived to be over 100 years old and smoked cigarettes and drank alcohol all of his or her life. Such a person simply got away with it. In the same way, not everyone who runs out into a busy road gets killed or injured, yet it is accepted that this is a dangerous thing to do.

If absolutely everyone who smoked died from a smoking-related medical condition, there would be no question in anyone's mind of it's potential harm.

But we are not all made the same and no doubt there are many predisposing factors, such as our genetic inheritance, that make some people resist the harmful effects of smoking while others succumb to its effects. Many of these effects are also related to the nutritional and mental health of a person, but there are many factors yet to be uncovered.

Smoking-related diseases

In 1989 the Royal College of Physicians (RCP) published figures showing that in that year nearly 40,000 people in the United Kingdom died from cancer of the lung. However, the most harmful effect of smoking is not on the lungs. In the same year, over 173,000 people died from ischaemic heart disease, which is recognized by the medical profession as a smoking-related disease.

The RCP publishes statistics on three principal medical conditions related to smoking, the third of which is bronchitis and emphysema. In 1989, the most up-to-date figures available at the time of writing this book, nearly 32,000 people in the UK died from these two closely related conditions. It should come as no surprise that cigarette smoke irritates the lungs and causes bronchitis, or that for some people this irritation will proceed to cancer. Those who had bronchitis that developed into cancer are excluded from the bronchitis death statistics. This means that in one country in one year around 72,000 people died from cancer of the lung, bronchitis or emphysema, almost directly related to smoking.

The effects of all this in terms of the costs to the NHS: days off work, time spent in seeing GPs and hospital consultants, the cost of travelling to see them, the time and cost of being in hospital for essential investigations and/or appropriate operations and the harrowing experience of being told one has cancer – all these things make me wonder why people still smoke.

Then there are the effects of the treatment itself. How many people do you know who have died from a form of cancer, despite the medical profession's best available efforts? How many of their remaining relatives, who watched their loved ones die, swear that they wished treatment had not been given because of the way the sufferers felt – sick, tired, no appetite, loss of hair on the head, etc? This does not happen to all patients who have treatment for cancer, but it does to all too many.

There are many other conditions that are either caused, triggered or aggravated by cigarette smoking. Anyone who has a stomach or duodenal ulcer should be helped to give up smoking immediately. Nicotine can cause a higher acid output in many people, although it can slow down the production of acid in others. I believe the latter is the main cause of peptic ulceration.

When food is swallowed its presence, touching the mucous membrane of the stomach, stimulates the production of acid to process foods. In smokers and in some people who take tea, coffee, alcohol and possibly other stomach irritants, I believe the ability of the stomach to produce acid is delayed so that there is a surge of acid half an hour or more after food has been swallowed, by which time it may have left the stomach and passed into the duodenum for its next phase of processing. This means that the acid produced in the stomach has no food to work on; not surprisingly, it burns a hole in the stomach lining, causing a peptic ulcer.

The way smoking causes heart problems is thought to be through its specific effects on arteries. Not only can the arteries supplying the heart muscles be affected, but also the peripheral arteries, ie those running to the limbs and the brain.

Intermittent claudication is a painful condition of the legs, very similar to angina of the heart. Smoking can damage the arteries supplying the lower limbs to such an extent that in some severe cases pain is produced by simply trying to walk from one room to another. The damage can eventually cause gangrene, which means either one or both legs have to be amputated or the person will simply die. One form of treatment for this, not commonly used in the United Kingdom, is intravenous infusions of EDTA, which is rather like having a chemical Dyno-rod down your arteries. It has to be done regularly if it is to help and can be dramatically effective. Anyone who suffers from this condition *must* give up smoking at once.

Nicotine can cause blood vessels to go into spasm, but a post-mortem study of people dying in Boston, Massachusetts, has shown that the more people smoked in life, the more advanced was the narrowing of their coronary arteries. Severe thickening of the small arteries supplying the heart was also found in these people. No wonder ischaemic heart disease is such a killer. This problem was found in 91 per cent of those who had smoked 40 cigarettes or more a day and in 48 per cent of those who had smoked less than 20 cigarettes a day. It was not found at all in non-smokers.

Another important observation has been made in a study of male and female industrial workers in northwest London. It was found that the blood of smokers had a significantly reduced ability to dissolve clots. As clots are being formed in the body in a small way all the time, this function is important. If the system is inefficient, a clot will form more easily. If it is in a heart artery it will cause a heart attack; if in the brain, it will cause a stroke.

Strokes are more common in smokers than in non-smokers. The greater likelihood of clotting and the spasm effect of nicotine can lead to irritability of the arteries, which will reduce the blood supply to the area. This alone can cause a stroke, or irregular heartbeats if it affects arteries leading to the heart muscle itself. If this progresses it can cause heart failure or a heart attack.

What the factor or factors are in cigarettes that cause all the harm is still under investigation. The main ingredients at present believed to be responsible for such medical problems are nicotine and carbon monoxide. Between 3 and 7 per cent of the haemoglobin of habitual smokers is converted into carboxyhaemoglobin, that is to say between 3 and 7 per cent of their blood is carrying, not oxygen as it should, but carbon monoxide, which is of no value to the body and may be positively harmful.

If a person already has reduced blood flow to the heart, limbs or brain caused by spasm of the blood vessels, extra clot formation and thickening of arterial walls, then any reduction in the oxygen content of the blood within the arteries will impose an additional strain on that tissue. No wonder it cannot cope. Furthermore, to compensate for this reduction in the oxygen-carrying capacity of the blood, the body may make more red blood cells. While this may increase the total amount of oxygen carried by the blood, the greater number of red blood cells makes the blood more 'sticky' and so clots can form more easily.

Whichever way you look at it, persistent smokers are constantly threatening their arteries and hence their lives.

Smoking and children

Children who smoke are a particular worry. Teen-agers who smoke suffer from respiratory disease more frequently and have more coughs than those who do not smoke. Some become short of breath on the slightest exertion. A knock-on effect is that they are absent from school because of pneumonia, bronchitis, catarrh and coughs, so their education may be adversely affected.

There is, moreover, good evidence that the non-smoking children of smoking parents have poorer health than children whose parents do not smoke. Respiratory infections are again the main problem, particularly in the first year of life, when bronchitis and pneumonia are in any case twice as common as in older children. By five years of age impaired lung function in smokers' offspring can often be demonstrated. Children of smoking parents, on average, do not grow up to be as tall as those of non-smoking parents, perhaps due to a wasting of zinc, which is so important to growth, somewhere in their metabolism as a result of the effects of passive smoking from a young age.

This clearly indicates how important it is to prevent children from ever starting to smoke and to try to explain to parents who smoke how much damage they are doing to their children.

Women smokers

Smoking adversely affects a woman's reproductive function. Women who smoke are either more likely to be infertile or may take longer to conceive than non-smoking women. An earlier menopause is likely in smokers. Once a woman is pregnant, a smoker has a small increased risk of a miscarriage, of bleeding sometime during pregnancy or of developing some kind of placental abnormality. The placentae of babies carried by women who smoke tend to be heavier, possibly as a compensation for the oxygen-lack due to the higher levels of carboxy-haemoglobin in their blood.

In fact the feature that has been statistically demonstrated to be most important in causing numbers of miscarriages is actually the number of cigarettes that the male of the partnership smokes; quite clearly, the more he smokes the more likely is his female partner to have a miscarriage. The male must therefore give up smoking well before his partner conceives, just as she ought to give up at least three months before planning a family. The future of their own children is at stake and parenthood should not be taken lightly.

It has been known for some time that babies born to women who smoke throughout pregnancy are on average ½lb (200g) lighter than those of non-smoking women. This observation has been made in many countries. It is possible that this is brought about by the poorer nutrition of smokers in comparison to non-smokers, but the evidence is not clear. Moreover, the offspring of women smokers have a slightly increased risk of perinatal death. The more the woman smokes, the greater the risk, which seems to be entirely explained by the consequences of low birth weight and placental abnormalities.

Women who smoke and take the contraceptive pill are abusing their bodies still further. Both smoking and the pill increase the risk of a heart attack, stroke or other cardiovascular conditions (such as migraine) in young women by three- to fourfold. When the two are combined there is an approximate tenfold increased risk, worse for women over 45 than for those under 35 years of age.

Passive smoking

Finally, there are the effects of breathing other people's smoke, known sometimes as passive smoking. Perhaps the best way of summarizing this is to report that an Australian court ruled, on 7th February 1991, that passive smoking causes lung cancer, asthmatic attacks and respiratory disease. This was the judgement in a case brought by the Australian Federation of Consumer Organisations against the Tobacco Institute of Australia, over an advertisement headed 'A Message From Those

Who Do . . . To Those Who Don't' which argued that 'there is little evidence and nothing which proves scientifically that cigarette smoke causes disease in non-smokers'.

After many expert epidemiologists and other doctors (most of them professors) from Australia, Britain, the USA and other countries had given their evidence of the harmful effects of passive smoking, Mr Justice Morling decided that there was overwhelming evidence for a 'cause and effect'. The tobacco group defending the action was not able to find any epidemiologist or other doctor to refute the argument. Its only defence was to try to break down the statistical evidence showing the effect. In his summing up, the judge said that 'the respondent [the tobacco industry] failed to call one witness whose special expertise is in Epidemiology and of whom it could be said that he "properly" held views contrary to those expressed by the distinguished Epidemiologists called by the applicant. It is a fair assumption, that such a witness would have been called by the respondent had he been available.'

There can be little doubt in anyone's mind now that the courts of law will rule that passive smoking can endanger people's health.

2
Mental attitude of smokers

All too often smokers decide for one reason or another to give up smoking but, when they do, their so-called withdrawal symptoms remind them continually of the day, the hour and the minute they smoked their last cigarette. They almost long for those wonderful days when they were happily smoking without any awareness of the harm smoking does.

Ex-smokers who simply had the common sense to give up nearly always feel that life was more pleasant, more fun and more relaxed when they were smoking; now it is just not the same. Quite a number (even very heavy smokers), however, give up smoking without the slightest whimper and wonder what all the fuss is about.

The majority of ex-smokers dwell on their problems. They envy those who continue to smoke, viewing them as the strong ones who have resisted the call to give it all up and who are still enjoying their smoking. These ex-smokers harp on about deprivation, the loss of their right to smoke, feeling that they have lost an essential friend, a necessary support through life's stresses and strains. In the past a cigarette always helped them get through an awkward situation, helped them think things through more clearly, helped them to concentrate. Or so they think.

Fear of withdrawal symptoms

Fear of experiencing the same problems seems to stop many people from giving up, or even making an attempt to give up. They have seen their friends try and fail. They have watched their happy, smoking friends give up and become bad-tempered, morose, restless and altogether unhappy. Some have put on a lot of weight, which makes them even unhappier. They have then watched the air of relief as these friends come back to work all happy again, back to their old sunny, chatty selves, although at the same time they are shame-faced at having been defeated and having had to go back to smoking.

Every smoker has heard others tell of the days, weeks, even months of a hard uphill struggle against withdrawal symptoms. They have all heard of the friend of a friend, formerly a strong, reliable, likeable person, who was transformed into an ill-mannered, ill-tempered individual by stopping smoking.

This is all nonsense. It does not need to be like that.

What I want you to do is to analyse your thoughts openly and honestly. Forget what others say or think. Ignore the possible bad side of things and look on the bright side. Realize what harm smoking is doing to you, or may do to you in due course. If you read Chapter 1, you may have learned some medical facts you weren't already aware of, but pictures of cancer of the lung do not seem powerful enough to put most smokers off. After all, not everyone who smokes gets cancer, so why should I be the unlucky one? You've heard it all before and you may well have tried to fool yourself. Well, now is the time to stop such pleasant delusions.

You must stop worrying about what all the *possible* dreadful effects of withdrawal are and start considering how you might easily have been misinformed about them. Start to assess what smoking is all about, why you are smoking, why you think you cannot give up, or why you think it might be hard for you to give up. Start to realize that all the old moans and complaints about withdrawal are really not necessary and may well not apply to you, nor need they apply to anyone for that matter.

Assume your cup is half full, rather than half empty. Think of all the benefits that will come your way from giving up. Read this book to the end and start to *understand* why smoking does you harm, what withdrawal symptoms are all about, why giving up smoking should be a piece of cake.

In many ways the next chapter, on addictions, should put it all into perspective; once you have read and understood it all, you should begin to recognize what your body is telling you. You will realize that your current belief that you 'need' or 'enjoy' your cigarette is simply false. Smoking is not necessary and, what is more, *there really is not any pleasure in it.*

Many people associate smoking with certain times of the day, at home in the evening, with a coffee at the end of a meal, during mid-morning or mid-afternoon breaks. They see a cigarette as a way of relaxing or winding down from various daily stresses. Once again, don't be fooled by this myth. When you read Chapter 4 you will recognize how wrong you are and that you are only relieving the symptoms induced by the previous cigarette in the first place.

Your Ball-and-Chain

Smoking is a ball and chain around your body, your whole way of life. Your whole existence at present revolves round your cigarettes. Making sure you have cigarettes and something to light them with at all times, wherever you are, wherever you are going, is often more important to you than your car-keys or your gloves. I remember one patient who told me he felt it was more important to ensure he had his cigarettes than to check he had his passport when going on holiday!

If you cannot manage without a cigarette (so you think), if you cannot go anywhere without double-checking you have enough cigarettes with you until you can get some more somewhere, your whole life is being controlled by your cigarette-smoking. Do you really accept that a pack of fags, with all the harm they are capable of doing you, should actually be in charge of your mind, your body and your whole life?

Think about it. Cigarettes control you at present. Once this has sunk in and you really do accept it, you have taken the first step towards giving up smoking. All through this book I will try to inform you and to help you understand what is happening to you at present, why you feel how you do, why you fear the thought of giving up, and why such fears are quite unnecessary.

I cannot promise that reading this book will definitely make you give up smoking for ever. No method is perfect, nor does any one method work for everyone. If the methods described in this book do not work for you, however, it won't be because you don't understand all about smoking.

If you cannot accept that cigarettes control you,

do not waste your time reading any further, unless you are simply intrigued to know what methods of giving up smoking I will be describing later. Perhaps, on second thoughts, if you do carry on reading you may understand more about your smoking habit and eventually accept that you are controlled by cigarettes after all.

How bad will it be?

Most smokers have already heard that withdrawal symptoms will be terrible. Before they even try to give up they are afraid of how bad the process will be, what it will do to them, how ill-tempered they will become, how much they will take it out on their family and friends. They have heard at least one friend say, 'I'm giving up cigarettes tomorrow – watch out for me!', and then they have watched the warning come true. Their friends (if they can actually remain on speaking terms with them) confirm what so many people have said all along about the effects of giving up smoking: 'It's terrible!', 'It's awful!', 'I feel ghastly!', 'It's like going through hell!'. All around are knowing nods from others who have been there before. How can anyone doubt that giving up smoking is hard and that it is to be expected that you will suffer?

The answer is that it needn't be bad. For many it may be incredibly simple. For some the difficulties may go on for a few days. It all depends upon you.

With all this background information of woe and despondency, what chance has anyone of giving up smoking without withdrawal symptoms occurring? If you start by expecting them, assuming they are inevitable, there is no way that they will not occur. Once even the slightest twinge begins, you will say to yourself, 'Oh, ho! Here they come!' You will exaggerate them out of all proportion in your own mind and will inevitably suffer. Hasn't everyone else?

'What did you expect?' will come from that voice inside your head. 'I told you so! Now get on and suffer!'

Forget about smoking for a moment and consider this analogy. Doctors have a great problem when they prescribe drugs. They know that side-effects can occur, but do not amount to much in most cases. Most people on medication experience no adverse effects at all. Yet, because they can occasionally occur, should doctors tell their patients of the *possible* adverse effects and perhaps frighten them so much that they won't take the prescribed drug?

The established adverse reactions to aspirin, for instance, are given in Figure 2.1. Despite this long list, literally thousands of tons of aspirin are taken by people the world over every year.

Some years ago a most interesting study was carried out. Hundreds of people were stopped in the

- The most common side-effects are headache, dizziness, ringing in the ears, visual and hearing difficulties, lassitude, drowziness, nausea, vomiting, diarrhoea, hyperventilation, mental confusion, tremor, restlessness, hallucinations, delirium, convulsions and coma, though these last four are not at all common.

- It is estimated that there are a total of a quarter of a million people in America who are hypersensitive to aspirin, and the symptoms are a profuse watery nasal discharge, swelling in any part of the body, extensive body itchy rash, asthma, swelling of the glottis, low blood pressure, shock, loss of consciousness and complete collapse.

- Most people who take aspirin regularly develop ulceration of the stomach or intestines and may pass blood in stools, and this can cause anaemia.

- Aspirin can compound male infertility. Chronic female users have babies of lower birth weight than normal. There is a definite increase in perinatal mortality, antepartum and postpartum bleeding, prolonged gestation and complicated deliveries.

- There is a tendancy for aspirin to cause bleeding through its effect on platelets, and it should definitely be avoided in people with severe liver damage, haemophilia and other bleeding tendencies. It must be stopped one week before being operated on.

- Aspirin can cause damage to the liver and kidney, recurring urinary tract infections, and a number of deaths are recorded every year from gastrointestinal bleeding and overdoses. There are over 10,000 cases of serious intoxication every year in USA.

Fig. 2.1: Established adverse reactions to aspirin

streets and asked if they suffered from headaches fairly frequently and, if so, would they be willing to participate in an experiment to test the effectiveness of the pain-relieving properties of an unnamed drug. Would they agree to take two tablets (which would be provided by the interviewer) the next time they had a headache and then report the effect?

The main purpose of the study was to try to find out how willing people would be to take a drug if they knew of its possible harmful effects. The interviewers had been instructed to tell interviewees about some of the known side-effects of that particular drug. One third (group A) were told about the mild adverse reactions that it might induce, with a vague mention that more serious reactions were a rare possibility. To a second third (group B) the mid-range adverse effects that might occur were stressed, while the more serious potential side-effects were emphasized to the final third (group C).

The results were quite simple in that those in groups B and C categorically refused to take part in the experiment. The vast majority of those in group A were generally reluctant to help, even though a small number said that they might participate. Possibly they thought they might be paid for joining the experiment.

The overwhelming response from people was, 'Why should I bother to take such a drug when I could simply take aspirin?' All the interviewees were then told that they had been asked to take part in a study about aspirin itself. They were not only amazed, but confessed that they were totally unaware that aspirin could be so potentially dangerous. It is impossible to say whether they would ever have taken an aspirin tablet if they had known what damage it can be capable of.

On the other hand, despite these potential dangers, some members of the medical profession regard aspirin as such a benefit that they are encouraging people to take the equivalent of between a quarter and a half of one aspirin tablet a day to prevent heart attacks in the future. Surely that is going to the other extreme!

The point of this slight digression is that if you know about the possible harmful effects of doing something, you are likely to think twice about doing it. We all know it is dangerous to cross the road, so we take care. If we don't, we might get hurt. Even if we don't take care, we might still not get hurt – we might simply get away with it.

If you think you know about the possible bad side-effects of giving up smoking, you are likely to hesitate over trying to give up. Even if you do make the attempt, you will probably be all pent up in apprehension of those withdrawal symptoms, not realizing that for you they are unlikely to be as bad as you have been told.

The issue of giving up smoking is obviously quite the opposite of the reactions to aspirin's side-effects observed in the interviewer experiment. In the latter, people were found to be happily taking aspirin when they had severe enough headaches, oblivious of the possible harm it could do and of course not experiencing any adverse effects at all. You, however, are afraid to stop doing something because you believe that you will feel awful if you do, when the chances are that you won't. Even if you do feel bad, in all probability the effects will not be as dreadful as you are expecting, and moreover will not last nearly as long as you think they will.

What I am saying is, in short: try to forget what you have heard. If you read on you will understand about withdrawal symptoms, what brings them on in the first place and what to do about them. If you understand them, accepting them will be all the easier. Not only should you be able to cope with them, but their effect upon you will be all the less.

Analyse your thoughts on smoking

Perhaps now would be a suitable time to sit back and analyse your thoughts about smoking. Sixteen questions about this are set out below; read each one carefully and ponder awhile. Be honest. Don't take any notice of what anyone else has told you about their problems, or the problems of a friend or relative. Instead, concentrate on yourself. You are you. You are unique. While you may have problems like other people, may look like your brother or have a similar feature or ideas on life to someone else, no-one, absolutely no-one, is exactly like you. So, for now, forget about everyone else around you and think only about how smoking affects you yourself.

1. Do I really *like* smoking?
2. Do I really *need* to smoke?
3. Am I aware of any harm it is doing to me at present?
4. Am I bothered about all the current available evidence of what harm smoking can do to me?
5. Do I actually know what harm smoking can do to me?
6. Do I accept current medical opinion about the harm smoking can do to me?
7. Do I actually care about current medical opinion on the harm smoking can do to me?
8. If I do accept and care about current medical opinion on the harm smoking can do to me, am I bothered about how it will affect my spouse or partner, my children, my family and friends if it makes me ill?
9. Do I care about the upset and inconvenience of hospital visiting which will be imposed upon my family and friends when I am admitted for investigation of a disease, caused by or an essential operation necessitated by my smoking?
10. Does it worry me about the strain it would put upon those I care for if I were to develop a stomach ulcer, have a heart attack, clog up the arteries in my

legs, or become so out of breath with bronchitis that I could be of no practical use to my family, my friends or myself?

11. Am I aware of the tragic effect that an early death from cancer of the lung could have upon my family?

12. Does it worry me that the taxes I pay on my tobacco simply go to pay for the treatment of other people who are now ill because they smoked and damaged their health?

13. Do I really feel that withdrawal symptoms are a justified reason for not trying to give up smoking?

14. Do I really feel that withdrawal symptoms are likely to be all that bad?

15. Am I only looking on the black side rather than considering the positive benefits to my health that giving up smoking will bring?

16. Do I realize that if I were to give up smoking, I would soon feel better?

3

Addiction, adaptation and withdrawal symptoms

Because giving up smoking can sometimes (but not always) lead to withdrawal symptoms, the whole of this chapter will be devoted to explaining what withdrawal symptoms are. The subject is quite complex, but much is known about it. Moreover, it is often not realized that people can be heavily addicted not only to smoking but also to foods and drinks that they consume every day.

The best known addictives are heroin, cocaine, crack, and so on: the street drugs that make such fortunes for their sellers and wreak such havoc upon the lives of addicts, and of course often kill them. Governments spend millions to try to stem the tide of illicit drugs, but in the end they will only disappear when people stop taking them. The same applies to smoking. After all, when the American government tried to ban alcohol in the prohibition era of 1920–34, the criminal underworld made fortunes because people carried on drinking illegally.

No matter how hard the government, the police and other authorities try to ban potentially harmful substances, in the end the decision on whether or not to take drugs comes from people themselves. If they refuse to buy or use them, no-one will be able to sell them. It's up to you – just don't buy cigarettes.

Adapting to stresses

In 1946 Hans Selyé, Professor of Experimental Medicine and Surgery at the University of Montreal in Canada, subjected a group of animals (usually rats) to various stresses, such as hunger, light, heat, cold and noise, and then observed the effects.

Professor Selyé noticed that if he continued the stress for quite a long time at a constant level, the animals' first reaction was to go into a state of shock. They would not eat, they did not clean themselves and they appeared altogether listless. This we refer to as Stage 1, or the stage of reaction.

If he continued the stress at a constant level the animals seemed to recover. They developed a second wind. They did not seem to mind the stress and seemed able to cope with it, as if they had somehow learned to adapt to the stress. This is referred to as Stage 2, or the stage of adaptation.

If, however, the stress was continued, there came a time when the animals suddenly seemed to give up and eventually died of adrenal and pituitary exhaustion. Before they died they seemed generally to become unwell and uninterested in life; they did not clean or care for themselves. This is *Stage 3*, or the stage of exhaustion.

Later, in 1956, Professor Adolph in New York repeated the experiments and also extended them by adding more stressing agents, such as certain foods and other potential allergens. What he found, in addition to confirming Hans Selyé's work, was that while some animals were made unwell by the stresses experienced at the various stages, they were not all equally affected. In fact some were hardly affected at all.

Adaptation in humans

If these reactions are extrapolated to human responses, this explains the phenomenon described by Dr Theron Randolph as 'specific adaptation syndrome'. In other words it simply means that humans, just like animals, respond in different ways to different stresses. Some manage well, some are affected slightly, some suffer badly. Each person is an individual and responds to life's forces individually, a fact that is rarely taken into account by orthodox doctors — who expect all people with schizophrenia, for example, to be the same, their illnesses all to have the same cause, and that they will all respond in exactly the same way to the various drugs available. However, humans and animals are just not all the same.

In Stage 1, then, a person may develop some symptoms when exposed to a potential allergen. Unfortunately, because of the nature of the 'reaction' and the time it takes to occur, it may not be obvious to the sufferer that it is a reaction to a food, a chemical or an environmental agent. Hence a cause may not be looked for. Such a reaction may be a headache, a rash, simply feeling unwell or tired, a bloated stomach, swollen ankles, palpitations for a few minutes, or an ache in a joint. In fact it could be anything that we tend to notice from time to time but which we brush off as 'just one of those things'. If we are fortunate, we are able to track down the offender. If not, our symptoms may become increasingly frequent. We are still in Stage 1.

Eventually, possibly after a short or a reasonably long time, the symptoms may disappear and we actually feel quite well. We may even start to cope better than before, seeming to be in a really good frame of mind and health. We are now in Stage 2.

Now that our bodies are coping well, tolerating the allergies or the stressing agents, we may not only feel well, but we may also have lost some of the symptoms we formerly suffered, even though we haven't actually done anything about them or know why they have gone. The disappearance of our reaction is again dismissed as 'just one of those things'. No-one has any idea why we are doing well and of course everyone is pleased if earlier complaints have 'vanished'. After all, who wants to be bothered or worry about nothing? It's gone, hasn't it? With any luck our bodies will continue to be able to adapt to the stimuli that were previously making us ill and we will stay in Stage 2 for the rest of our lives.

In fact, because it is extremely difficult for us to avoid pollution, chemicals in our food and food sensitivities, especially if we are unaware that they are harming us or if we don't know how to isolate and avoid them, it is ideal if we can stay permanently in Stage 2. This means that our adaptive mechanisms are functioning well and are able to tolerate life's stresses and strains. In other words, we are very much in tune with the modern world and all it throws at us.

It is in fact amazing how well our bodies do cope and how few of us are truly unwell, even though most of us have some problems from time to time. The trouble is that we are throwing so much rubbish at our bodies in what we eat and drink, and moreover are having it thrown at us by the pollution in the atmosphere and the chemicals we blithely use every day of our lives – such as hairsprays, polishes, etc, which we feel we can no longer live without – that sooner or later our bodies give up. They simply cannot tolerate it all for ever.

Entering Stage 3

Sooner or later something gives and we enter Stage 3, when our ability to adapt finally says: 'I can't manage any longer. I have tried all this time, but it's all getting too much for me. I've had it!' Now the start of something more serious is apparent, although the symptoms may be intermittent. Our bodies can still tolerate a great deal, but they are showing the signs of strain more and more often.

What actually causes us to enter Stage 3 varies from person to person. It may be something that almost passes unnoticed, rather like the single straw that breaks the camel's back, but it is likely to be something more serious, even though its importance at the time may go unrecognized.

More obvious reasons for entering Stage 3 may perhaps be an illness (even flu); an operation; a bereavement; losing a job; being forced to take on unwanted responsibilities at work; or being passed over for promotion, with all the attendant disappointment. Other possible triggers might be moving house; the strain of supporting a close friend who has lost a loved one; the death of the family pet; a car accident; a disastrous holiday, with delays at an airport or the problems resulting from lost luggage.

For many young couples the first baby, with all the inevitable worries and lack of sleep, may cause either the mother or father to enter Stage 3. The mother is the one most likely to be affected, particularly if she has not looked after her nutritional health during pregnancy, when the demands made on her body by the baby inside her have been particularly great. Breast-feeding is also very demanding on nutrition, time and sleep patterns.

Stage 3 is the stage when the adaptive mechanisms have started to wear out and addictive mechanisms are in play. The symptoms experienced in Stage 1 return but are now just as often caused by avoiding the allergen as by taking it, which may make it far more difficult to identify the reasons for their occurrence. For example, a headache may occur not only if too much coffee is drunk, but also if the patient does not have a cup of coffee for a number of hours. Many coffee-drinkers know that a cup too close to bedtime will disturb their sleep, so they do not drink coffee after, say, 8pm or 9pm. That means they refrain from coffee for 10 to 12 hours until the next morning, when they wake up with a headache which they can then relieve with their first cup of coffee of the morning.

This is a known problem with all addictions, which is a feature of Stage 3. *Symptoms occur on withdrawal of the allergen and can be relieved by taking a dose of that allergen.* Many people have observed this effect without fully realizing its significance. How many people come home after a day out literally gasping for a cup of tea? A cup may be refreshing for some people, or a way of relaxing after a long walk, but nevertheless this response could be indicative of an addiction to tea. Again many people, women in particular, say that they *need* two cups of tea just to get going in the morning.

How many people literally crave chocolate at times, especially women in the week before their period starts? How often do people dive into the refrigerator for a hunk of cheese? Every day people satisfy their addiction to sugar, sweets, biscuits, crisps, cakes, coffee, tea, cola drinks, cheese and many other foods and drinks usually of no nutritional value, without knowing that they may be harming themselves.

It takes courage to give up something your body is craving, especially when it has never occurred to you that it might be doing you harm. No-one has ever suggested it before. Your doctor doesn't know of it, was never taught it at medical school and is hardly likely to read about in medical journals, which concentrate more on the drug treatment of disease.

How often have you seen a cantankerous, stroppy, hyperactive child ruin his or her parents' day out shopping, ignoring parental pleas to behave, embarrassing them and yet not caring? The child constantly asks for sweets, chocolate or a bag of crisps and will not behave or be consoled until the parents finally give in. Then the child's whole demeanour rapidly changes, becoming all sweetness and light and allowing the adults to start enjoying their day.

Here is a classic picture of a child becoming hyperactive and generally obnoxious not so much because of being unable to have his or her own way (although that may be a factor), but more likely because the child is suffering from hypoglycaemia (to be discussed in Chapter 5) or because of withdrawal symptoms from the last 'high' caused by the previous sugary food or drink. The relenting parents satisfy the low blood sugar or food craving, the child's blood sugar is raised and the symptoms settle, only to return again in due course.

The pattern is so clear that it amazes me that more doctors don't recognize it for what it is. It is usually the patient or the parents, advised by a friend or having read an article in a newspaper or magazine or having seen it described on television, who start to push their doctors to recognize the possibility of a food or environmental allergen and persuade them to help by following this approach. Doctors are commonly the last people to realize how important the role of such allergens can be and often give it scant thought, largely because their training never covered such a topic and, anyway, they have no idea how to follow it up.

In the case of adults with long-term addictions to foods and chemicals, Stage 3 can make a person very unwell and may include signs that the person is dying. Hardening of the arteries or lung cancer will eventually catch up with the person, but it is never too late to try to do something. The alternative is to succumb to the condition or at least to become increasingly unwell.

The stages of reaction, adaptation and exhaustion can be illustrated by three fairly common examples, which you may not have viewed in this way before.

The Bunion

When you wear a bad-fitting shoe, Stage 1 is the blister with its pain and discomfort, the sore red area where the rubbing occurs. The top layer of skin may separate from the layer beneath and inflammatory fluid may collect inbetween. The whole area is most uncomfortable. It is the body's response to the friction of the leather on the skin where the two don't fit well together.

Because of the pain, it is likely that you will protect the blister with a plaster, or take the shoe off to ease the discomfort. As you must wear shoes, you will probably go back to your old ones for a few days or, if this is not possible because you have thrown the old ones away, you put up with the pain which is anyway now less, because of the protective plaster you have applied.

The friction continues, even through the plaster. Over a period of time you enter Stage 2 as you develop a thick piece of skin where the original blister was. This is the body's response to the continual rubbing, as Hans Selyé originally described. Your skin learns to compensate and put up with, or tolerate, the continual rubbing and you do not notice any discomfort any more.

This is a classic Stage 2: no symptoms of note, although if you examine your foot you will observe the hard skin as evidence of your body's adaptive response. This is unlike reactions to foods and chemicals, where there is usually no observable sign that you are adapting, so you are unaware of the state you are in and thus there is nothing much you can do about it.

Stage 3 is entered only if the shoe cannot adapt to the shape of the foot and the rubbing continues on the same spot. As happened to Hans Selyé's experimental animals, your body cannot continue to tolerate the friction for ever and the adaptive mechanisms will eventually break down. In this situation the centre of the hard skin breaks and you develop an infected bunion, finally forcing you to do something about the problem.

It might be argued that this example is to some

extent inappropriate, as there is no sign of an addiction developing. You don't actually *want* to put the shoe on to give the hard piece of skin a nice rub! Nevertheless, the principles are the same and the example illustrates the gradual development of the three stages.

The Alcoholic

If you have never drunk alcohol before, your first drink will most likely make your head swim. You may feel sick or actually be sick and as well as feeling generally ill, you may find that your social behaviour becomes uninhibited and that you giggle. You may also become sleepy. The degree to which the symptoms develop will depend upon how much you drink, how strong the alcohol content is, how cheap the drink is (the more chemicals mixed in the drink, the worse the effect) and whether or not you had anything in your stomach at the time you took the drink.

This is clearly Stage 1, where your body is reacting to the drink and showing it doesn't like the effect, although, unfortunately, some people do like the effect and are not put off by these symptoms.

Because it is socially acceptable to drink alcohol in moderation, most people take an alcoholic drink every so often and find that their tolerance level has increased. Some find that they can have a few drinks without any noticeable adverse effect, or possibly only minor tolerable ones, even though their blood alcohol level may be legally over the driving limit. They have, of course, now entered Stage 2.

This is an interesting feature of great clinical significance, because there may be laboratory proof that you should be drunk and yet few clinical features to confirm this condition. A 'new' drinker, on the other hand, may feel drunk despite having a very low blood alcohol level. The difference seems to lie in the way that one's tissues react to a given level of alcohol in the bloodstream. Once again this highlights the significance of individuality and Dr Theron Randolph's idea of individual susceptibility.

The average drinker may appear temporarily to return to Stage 1 if he or she suddenly starts drinking above their tolerance level, perhaps as a result of the loss of a job, a bereavement, the break-up of a marriage, or a similar crisis. Such drinkers who try to find refuge in drink, drowning out thier sorrows, develop all the symptoms of Stage 1 again because of this heavy drinking. They may even be sick in the pub toilet but, because their personal problems have not yet been solved, continue to drink.

If the situation remains the same, Stage 2 is reached, but this time at a higher level. The drinker soon finds that continuing to drink excessively produces little noticeable effect and is able to put away an amount of drink that would make most people decidedly ill. If, however, the drinker's problems are resolved and the drinking stops, the matter will end there. After a suitable period of time the drinker's alcohol tolerance level will return to its original level.

Although the majority of adults (and many teenagers) drink alcohol periodically, they very seldom ever become alcoholic unless they embark on the round of excessive drinking caused by problems such as business pressures. Nevertheless, there is no doubt that temporary excessive alcoholic intake can have an appalling effect upon some people, the worst being the temper that develops in some men who then batter their wives, only to become extremely upset when they sober up and realize what harm they did when they were so drunk.

Stage 3 tends to develop in relation to very heavy drinking over a long period, usually when a personal problem has gone on for some time, so that the drinking has become a habit. Even if the problem is solved, it may be difficult for the drinker to stop drinking, because he or she starts to feel unwell when alcohol is avoided. That is to say, there are painful withdrawal symptoms.

Thus Stage 3 has begun around the time when the poor sufferer starts to *need* to drink alcohol more and more frequently in order to keep feeling reasonably well, although in fact the drinker would admit to never feeling well at all, simply to feeling worse when not drinking.

The longer a person at this stage goes without a drink, the worse he or she feels. Having finally managed to go to sleep, with the aid of quite a large intake of alcohol, the drinker will then sleep heavily, but feel awful in the morning, because refraining from alcohol for those hours of sleep means waking up with a mixture of a hangover and withdrawal symptoms. The sufferer can at least partially ease some of these symptoms by having some alcohol, but in the long run is on the rapid downhill trail.

In the early part of Stage 3 there is probably little actual awareness that things are going wrong, although drinkers who are honest with themselves, if such people exist, would probably admit to drinking a bit more often than before, possibly starting earlier in the day, and may also accept that the drinks give them a lift of sorts. Even if they do not admit all this, those around them notice, so clearly the alcohol *is* having an effect upon their metabolism.

There is seldom ever a sudden onset of any stage; the progression may be almost imperceptible from one day to another. Certainly in Stage 3 (the stage of addiction), the addictive features appear gradually and it may be appropriate to say that Stage 3 has become firmly established when the drinker finds he or she cannot start the day or get going without the usual drink. The withdrawal symptoms, caused by refraining from alcohol while asleep, need to be eased by 'the hair of the dog'.

While most people would recognize these symptoms in relation to alcohol, how often might they also apply to some extent to items like tea or coffee, chocolate or cheese? The addictive pattern can apply to these 'foods' just as much (albeit to a less damaging extent) as to poisonous alcohol.

All alcoholics are in Stage 3 and their whole systems are in a thoroughly addictive condition. It amazes me how anyone succeeds in 'drying out' from alcohol when they are exposed while in a special unit to equally addictive substances such as cigarettes, tea, coffee, sugar and white flour products.

Noise

Although it is not a substance like a food, a drink or a drug, the effect of noise on humans can be used as a further example of this whole process, even if it lacks some of the essential elements. It is also interesting because it was one of the stresses that Hans Selyé first applied to his experimental animals in order to test their reactions.

In human terms noise has sometimes been used as a form of torture. Like anything that is overdone, it can be very damaging. If humans are exposed to a constant excessive noise, even if they find it tolerable, how do they respond?

We all react to different so-called everyday noises according to what we are used to. A person who lives in a quiet country village might find it hard to become accustomed to the noise of a major city and at first would not sleep well. On arriving in town, therefore, Stage 1 would probably be a headache from 'all the noise'; the person would probably be bad-tempered or irritable and would almost certainly not sleep well for the first few nights at least.

Thus Stage 1 would be reached almost immediately. However, it is amazing how quickly people can get accustomed to such a change, so long as they are in the right frame of mind. A country student, excited about going to a big, new, city university, would most likely settle in very well and Stage 2, the stage of adaptation, would soon be achieved. If, on the other hand, the country-living student were a quiet, introverted type, who was anxious about whether he or she was going to be able to cope away from home for the first time and possibly not even sure if the right university course had been selected, then Stage 2 might never be reached and the Stage 1 effect might be sufficiently severe to make the student give it all up and go home. In that case, of course, there would be other stresses at work as well as the noise.

The two ways of looking at the response to such a new environment — one by an excited, optimistic, extroverted 18-year-old, the other by a timid, introverted, anxious person – is very much what Professor Selyé noticed and what Dr Theron Randolph applied to humans when he talked about individual susceptibility. We all react to different situations in our own way.

What of the effect of either a piece of noisy machinery on a worker, or loud music on a youngster? The worker, when first exposed to excessive noise in the workplace, will initially find the environment hard to tolerate, go home with a headache, sleep badly for a number of nights and probably be a bit bad-tempered.

Depending on the worker's job, home life and the presence or absence of any particular other stresses, he or she may soon come to find the noise quite tolerable and will rapidly enter Stage 2. This position may be maintained for many years and, of course, good management may install quieter machinery, or provide either sound-boxes over the noisy equipment or ear protectors. Thus the noise stress will disappear and the problem will be solved.

If no solution to the noise is found, Stage 3 is likely to take the form of the worker becoming physically affected by starting to go deaf. The damage will occur gradually but, after a time, someone will notice that he or she is asking for remarks to be repeated more often than is reasonable and finally it will become obvious that there is a hearing problem.

Teenagers seem to love loud music and the pure volume they favour can be painful to their parents' ears. Stage 1 is passed very quickly because they are determined to enjoy the bright lights, the atmosphere of the music, and this enhances the body's ability to adapt. There is never any suggestion of wearing ear-plugs or muffs. In addition, any conversation has to be shouted above the music.

There is evidence that some teenagers are themselves entering Stage 3 and are starting to go deaf, so their loud music could eventually leave them with a permanent disability. At first it is the extremes of the hearing range that are usually affected; some people losing the high ranges first, others the lower ranges. Others suffer an across-the-board loss.

With most Stage 3 effects there is an addictive element, but not really in relation to noise. The music-lover will, of course, need the music to be played at a louder volume in order to be able to hear, ie to have the desired effect. This need of *more sound* may be rather like an addiction, but it is not necessary to have the music *more often*. On the other hand, if deaf people cannot understand what others are saying this may be compared to with-drawal symptoms – withdrawal of sound from their lives.

If you avoid the persistant excessive sound of the workplace machinery or loud music once you are in Stage 3, whether or not you recover your hearing will depend upon a number of factors, the most important being the degree of damage that has already taken place. This damage will have been sustained by the auditory nerve, which means that hearing aids will not be nearly so effective as in cases of deafness through other causes. As the nerve is absolutely vital to the act of hearing, any damage to it may be irreversible.

4

Smoking addiction

People generally start to smoke as teenagers, occasionally even younger. They very seldom begin once they have become adults, for by then they realize what a bad habit it is.

At whatever age a person smokes a cigarette for the first time, it always produces symptoms, such as light-headedness or a dizzy feeling, palpitations, headache, nausea and a cough. Usually all of these reactions occur, although some may be more of a problem than others.

The fact that everyone, without exception, suffers in this way means that tobacco-smoking is not a true allergy, as an allergy is said to affect only a minority of people. Rather, it must have a toxic effect, for no-one escapes these symptoms with their first cigarette. Nevertheless, the effects of tobacco in Stages 1, 2 and 3 make it an ideal example to describe against the background detail of addictions in general which was given in Chapter 3.

Smoking Stage 1

Stage 1 symptoms of smoking are those uncomfortable reactions described above, perhaps experienced when a young person first smokes behind the bicycle-shed at school, or somewhere else that is away from prying adult eyes. However, smoking is usually started either as a 'dare' or to appear adult or sophisticated. Whatever the reason for young people starting to smoke, there are generally pressures of one sort or another to try it again and again, just to keep up with their peer group. The extraordinary thing is that under normal circumstances such an unpleasant experience would undoubtedly mean that the first cigarette would be the last. No-one should ever have another cigarette after feeling so wretched with the first one.

So many children have seen their parents or other adults smoking, or watched someone smoking in a film, that it is easy for them to think that smoking is something that adults 'do'. Most sensible adults, of course, hope their children will never take up the filthy habit they themselves wish they had never taken up in the first place. Parents may even achieve their ambition of putting their children off the idea by offering them that first cigarette on some special occasion, like a party or at Christmas. In the absence of peer-group pressure the young person will probably freely admit that the symptoms are disgusting and he or she may even (we hope) be very sick, especially if the parents push their child to keep smoking on this occasion.

If this whole experience is horrible enough – and it usually is – there will be no question of these young people trying cigarettes again. In fact, they are so appalled at the unpleasant taste and the dreadful effects that tobacco has on them that they turn on their parents, finding it impossible to understand why they appear to 'enjoy' smoking and why they still smoke at all. They do not yet realize what a problem an addiction is and, with any luck, they will never experience it themselves.

If, on the other hand, teenagers smoke a cigarette for the first time when in the company of their peers, the outcome may be quite different. The first cigarette ought to put them off for a long time, if not for life, but unfortunately the pressure of the group may produce the opposite effect.

Smoking Stage 2

As Hans Selyé showed so many years ago, periodically trying something that is capable of producing symptoms will lead to a degree of tolerance, which of course is Stage 2. In due course smoking every so often gradually has less adverse effects upon the teenager. Others in the group say, 'There you are! We told you you'd soon get used to smoking.' And this is in fact the case. The young person's body learns to tolerate the effect of nicotine, because it has a great ability to cope with much of life's stresses and strains.

This capacity to tolerate is absolutely essential to human survival and our bodies do their best to apply it to things which we cannot avoid as well as to those with which we deliberately contaminate our bodies, although they may give us warning signs of problems. Each of us should realize that we ought to take responsibility for our own health wherever and whenever possible, but all too often we reject what our bodies are trying to tell us. Far too often we write a problem off as 'just one of those things' and leave it to the fates or the doctors!

Thus Stage 2 in smoking is reached when a person continues to smoke but seems not to suffer from any particular ill-effects. Because it is a potential throat irritant, smoking will make a sore throat or a cold worse, but very often smokers put up with this extra discomfort, although they may give up temporarily. Unfortunately, when they feel better they often start smoking again without thinking – simply taking up the habit once more.

Smoking Stage 3

As with all addictive substances, it is difficult to say when exactly Stage 3 begins. In many people it may be as a result of an infection, a bereavement, the loss of a job, or simply extra unwanted responsibilities at work. Something as everyday as moving house could be the precipitating factor, or just being overtired for one reason or another. Many others, however, may move into Stage 3 for no specific reason.

Whether or not there is a reason for the onset of Stage 3 the body's reaction is the same. Its ability to keep tolerating simply starts to wear out. It can no longer put up with the constant effects of the many chemicals in cigarette smoke, all of which are potentially harmful, and sooner or later the adverse effects are bound to show.

Research workers can show the harmful effects that any one of these chemicals can have upon an animal over a lifetime, or over a shorter time if larger doses are given. They can clearly demonstrate the much worse effects of testing two of these chemicals together. Indeed, the overall effect is often more than the sum of the individual effects, which are in fact usually multiplied. As cigarette smoke contains over 100 chemicals, it is impossible to say what the multiplication factor of the adverse effects of these chemicals is likely to be. The fact that so many people get away with so much for so long is a clear indication of how capable the body is of adapting, but this cannot go on for ever.

In Stage 2 a person tends to smoke as a habit,

or simply when offered a cigarette at a party, for example. Stage 3 can be said to have arrived when the smoker starts to crave a cigarette. Certain habits develop and a smoker may casually smoke with a cup of tea or coffee after each meal, at each mid-morning or mid-afternoon break, or when sitting down with an early evening drink after getting home from work.

Some busy people simply develop the habit of smoking when doing things like writing or trying to solve a problem. The average non-addicted smoker may smoke 10 cigarettes a day simply out of habit, while those who smoke when busy may smoke up to 20 a day. In Stage 2, however, smoking is clearly a habit and people can often easily break the habit and not smoke at a particular time if their life changes for a day or so, without suffering at all or even noticing that they have not smoked all day.

In Stage 3 this habit starts to become a need and a degree of craving or compulsion to smoke develops. It is all subconscious to begin with, but although it is at first unnoticed, this feeling is nontheless there, whether or not the smoker admits it. He or she is simply aware of thoughts such as: 'Where are my cigarettes?', or: 'I mustn't go out without my cigarettes'. Later, anxiety develops at the thought of not having any cigarettes about one's person.

Coupled with the need for a cigarette, a set of

symptoms gradually develops when the smoker has not smoked for a while. These early withdrawal symptoms take the form of just not feeling right, being slightly uncomfortable and fidgety, finding it a little difficult to get on with things. Many of the early symptoms are manifested just as a 'feeling' about something which is extremely difficult to describe or define. As the withdrawal symptoms become more obvious, this feeling turns into an anxiety and smokers become more obviously concerned about how they feel. They are certainly starting to be worried.

Once in Stage 3, the early or moderate symptoms can be relieved by smoking a cigarette and by doing so the person feels better. This relief of withdrawal symptoms is a cardinal feature of the early part of Stage 3, whatever the person is addicted to. It is often portrayed graphically in film and on television in relation to heroin, when the addict's abject misery is soon relieved by a dose or a fix.

I fully accept that many of my patients fear how bad the withdrawal symptoms from smoking may be and for this reason they may take a long time making up their minds to try to stop. There is no such problem when I ask them to give up tea or coffee. Half the time this fear is quite unwarranted; if they were only to try to stop, after having had a reasonable explanation of all that is involved in addiction and what withdrawal symptoms are, they would find it not nearly as difficult as they had thought. Fear of the unknown is always worse than fear of the understood, which is why the aim of this book is to try to make the whole problem of smoking so clear that you will have no fear at the thought of giving up.

In some respects, Stage 3 of smoking could conveniently be divided into Stage 3A and Stage 3B. In Stage 3A, the early symptoms of withdrawal are first just a feeling and then become very obvious. However, they are not incapacitating. In Stage 3B, however, the smoker still craves a cigarette and develops all the symptoms of withdrawal, but things start to become a problem. The withdrawal symptoms were tolerable before, but now they are stronger than ever and can be really unpleasant. The person becomes bad-tempered and unpleasant to live or work with unless he or she has a cigarette.

More importantly still, the craving and other withdrawal symptoms are not relieved as fully as before, so the sufferer may continue to suffer. In addition, the smoker needs to smoke more frequently to achieve only a small measure of relief. True addiction to smoking has been reached when the fix is needed more often and in greater amounts in order to achieve even some relief.

Finally, to make matters even worse, the smoker's health begins to suffer. Concentration becomes impossible without a cigarette. A persistent cough develops, or even bronchitis, and the smoker gets short of breath on the least exertion, such as climbing stairs. If you were in such a condition and you were able to look inside your arteries and your heart, you would see the damage being done by the chemicals you inhale so many times every day. Any one of the conditions mentioned in Chapter 1 could be developing. Without any doubt, smoking is a killer. The only uncertainty is as to which cause of death will strike first: lung cancer, a heart attack or a stroke.

Which stage are you at?

The three stages, Stage 1 of reaction, Stage 2 of adaptation and Stage 3 when the adaptive mechanisms start to fail, are very important to an understanding about giving up smoking. If you are still in Stages 1 or 2, which you may still be, giving up will not be at all difficult. In fact your body will breathe a sigh of relief and you will rapidly feel better.

If you are not yet in Stage 3, reading this book should give you an added incentive to give up and should help you to understand what is in store for you if you do not. My advice is: GIVE UP AS SOON AS YOU HAVE FINISHED READING THIS BOOK ALL THE WAY THROUGH.

If you are in Stage 3, it is to be hoped that you

are only in the early stage, but even if you are in Stage 3b it is not too late. <u>It is never too late</u>; if you thought that it was, the chances are that you would not be reading this book. The fact that you are means that you want to stop smoking and hope that my approach will help you.

So keep on reading. There are more explanations to come and there is much you can do for yourself to help you break your addictive pattern. In the end it is a full understanding of the whole problem and what to do about it that will not only convince you it is worthwhile trying to stop, but will also help you to stop.

5
Hypoglycaemia
and smoking

Hypoglycaemia means low blood sugar. You may wonder why it is being discussed in a book about stopping smoking, but I believe the link between this condition and tobacco addiction to be of over-whelming significance.

Symptoms of hypoglycaemia

While the symptoms of hypoglycaemia classically occur as a result of a particularly low level of blood sugar, similar or the same symptoms can result when the level of blood sugar is nearly normal but has fallen from a point that was very high, that is to say that a rapid fall in blood sugar can lead to hypoglycaemic symptoms.

The classic features are light-headedness, dizzi-ness, fatigue, hunger, a need to eat something that is akin to the desire to binge, sweating, palpitations, mental confusion, anxiety, weakness and a sense of unease. Aren't these symptoms similar to the ones a smoker suffers from when giving up smoking? More serious symptoms that can occur when a person's blood sugar is low include behavioural disorders – sometimes amounting to outright aggression or criminal acts – frequent headaches, epileptic attacks and depression. Might there be a connection with the fact that police and social workers will often tell you that criminal acts, especially ones of violence, can be committed 'out of the blue'? When the perpetrator is interviewed later, often after a cigarette or a cup of sweet tea or coffee, he or she seems calm and rational and highly unlikely to have commited such an offence.

Numerous studies in prisons and detention centres in the USA have shown how arguments and acts of violence towards other inmates have tended to occur before meals, or late at night, or early in the morning after 10 or 12 hours without food. These studies have also clearly demonstrated how a change in the diet can drastically change these abnormal behaviour patterns.

Most people who suffer from hypoglycaemia do so shortly after a meal, often around an hour and a half after eating. All the symptoms described above can occur, although generally only some of them are experienced. Eating more food, especially sugary foods, rapidly relieves the symptoms. This, under-standably, makes sufferers feel that they *need* that food, that they *must have it* or they will be ill. They feel wretched, down in the dumps, hungry, not at all well, unable to think properly or concentrate. Again, note how similar these symptoms are to those that may be experienced during the withdrawal phase from smoking. So it is not surprising that hypoglycaemia sufferers will eat something sweet if they have earlier discovered that it will make them feel better and get rid of these awful symptoms.

Understandable though this may be, you are only fooling yourself if you act like this. The relief is only temporary and in the long run it may be part of your downfall, if it has not already become so. The reasons for this are explained below and are important because an understanding of hypoglycaemia, as of addictions generally, will help you to give up smoking.

Sugar

Unfortunately, most doctors do not understand that hypoglycaemia is the result of a lifetime of having too much sugar and refined carbohydrate. Low blood sugar is a rebound from a high level produced by an excessive intake of sugary foods in the first instance. Yet, in orthodox medical terms, hypoglycaemia is thought only to occur in an established diabetic who has injected too much insulin without following that by eating a meal. Although there are of course many inter-related factors, the chief cause of hypoglycaemia is in fact simply over-indulgence in sugar and refined carbohydrate. Attention to this aspect of your diet will reap great rewards and certainly play a part in your effort to stop smoking.

Most people believe that sugar provides energy and that by pumping it into the blood (via the food that they eat), their blood sugar levels will be kept up and they will be energetic all the time. Sadly, this is far from the truth. Athletes are now discovering that they can perform far greater feats if refined carbohydrate is *not* part of their diet; in fact if they do eat it they notice that their performance is below their best.

Confectionery and soft-drinks manufacturers' advertisements often hint at the energy-giving prop-erties of their products and it has to be recognized that under certain circumstances this claim is true. Those circumstances are when a person's blood sugar has fallen to a low point, nearly always as a rebound from having had some sugar or similar food a short time – between one and three hours – earlier. This point cannot be stated often enough and I do not apologize for repeating it. Many people feel very hungry a short time after a meal, even though that meal satisfied them at the time and should have lasted them for many hours.

Evolution and diet

To understand how hypoglycaemia develops in a person, we need to go back two million years or so to see how human physiology was evolved in relation to the foods that were available then. As 'civilization' was not yet developed, our Stone Age ancestors did not sit down to meals as we understand them today. Rather, they would have eaten what they could find when they found it, although there may have been some sort of code of behaviour for the males to take food home to the females and children, unless these family groups moved around together.

Archaeological studies have shown that these early people did eat meat, fish and eggs but that they were probably gatherer-hunters, which means that most of what they ate was whatever was readily available. Thus our ancestors' diet would most likely have been largely vegetarian and would have consisted mainly of fruits, seeds, nuts, berries, leaves, grasses and roots, the latter being the forerunners of potatoes, carrots and similar foods that we eat today. While people would at some time have developed sufficiently organized groups to collect, distribute and store certain foods, for much of the time two million years ago they would simply have eaten the foods as soon as they found or caught them.

Part of our forebears' daily lives would have been spent in hunting and trying to kill animals, which would either have been eaten raw where they died or taken to a suitable place, some sort of camp site, where the meat would have been cooked after fire had been discovered. If they lived near a river or stream they would have learned the art of fishing in some crude way, either by 'tickling' or spearing. They would certainly have raided nests for eggs, which were probably in abundance.

Most archaeological studies indicate that our earliest ancestors came originally from the warmer parts of the world, such as Africa or Australia. Survival in the colder regions would have been difficult then, so any early peoples who evolved in those areas at this time could well have died during the winter, either from lack of food or from the cold. Even in the areas where we have found human remains from all those years ago, there would still have been easy deaths, from marauding animals and fights, for instance. Various natural disasters like floods, droughts, volcanoes and possibly disease could easily have reduced the already small numbers of humans stil further.

Despite all the problems that confronted a developing species, the food that was available was natural and uncontaminated by modern drugs (chiefly antibiotics and hormones), pesticides, fertilizers and all the paraphernalia of intensive animal farming and high-turnover food-marketing. Our forebears certainly never had artificial colourings, preservatives or other unnatural chemicals added to their food. Moreover, there was no sugar, wheat, corn or any of today's grains, although our early ancestors may well have eaten some grasses or found a liking for honey. These would have been taken only very occasionally. At some point, probably 100,000 years ago at the most, milk from goats or sheep may have become available.

Thus the diet of our distant ancestors was very different from ours today. The physiology and biochemistry of the human body developed according to what was available in the form of food and the existing environment. This hardly altered at all over two million years or thereabouts, the first significant change (after the discovery of fire) being the development of agriculture. This began only about 40,000 years ago and became reasonably established within 30,000 years, ie about 10,000 years ago. During this time the Egyptians learnt to grow and store wheat, while the Orientals established rice crops. This meant that food was available all the year round, although it was food of a different sort to that which had been available earlier. A population explosion of sorts took place and 'civilization' began.

This discussion of the habits of early humans may seem to be a digression, but the point I want to make — which is central to my theme of hypogly-caemia and its relationship to smoking — is that, among all the changes in our diet over the centuries, two of the most important 'foods' we now eat were never available when human physiology and biochemistry were developing. These are sugar and refined carbohydrate. In a non-diabetic person, hypoglycaemia only develops if too much of these substances have been consumed over a lifetime.

The time it takes for hypoglycaemia to develop varies from person to person. It can be very obvious in the bad behaviour of a hungry child who reverts to smiles and a sunny temperament after starting to eat a meal. On the other hand it may not appear until adulthood, when depression becomes the principal outward sign of the problem. *There is no doubt whatsoever in my mind that many smokers suffer from hypoglycaemia and that hypoglycaemia is part of the withdrawal symptoms that develop when they try to stop smoking.*

Our physiology then and now

Figure 5.1 illustrates the development of the human diet, from our earliest days to the twentieth century. The meat, fish and eggs our distant ancestors ate when available contained mainly protein, but in an uncontaminated form. Their carbohydrate intake would have come from fruits, berries, seeds, plants

Diet of Paleolithic people
(1–2 million years ago)

MAINLY	NUTS	FRUITS	SEEDS	GRASSES
	ROOTS	PLANTS	BERRIES	LEAVES
POSSIBLY	HONEY	MEAT	FISH	EGGS
		(+ bone marrow)		

Human physiology was based on this largely vegan diet.

Diet of Homo Sapiens
(40,000–10,00 years ago)

WHEAT   by Egyptians
RICE   by Orientals

During this time, the period when agriculture developed, people's average height diminished, only to increase when more meat was eaten in recent centuries.

Diet of modern humans

COW'S MILK AND MILK PRODUCTS

Not readily available to the masses (especially town-dwellers) until about a century ago. There has been a massive increase in daily consumption of milk and milk products since the Second World War, when farmers were told to become self-sufficient in food.

SUGAR

Probably introduced in the time of Queen Elizabeth I, but not generally available until the late 1800s. Sugar-containing foods now dominate Western diets.

CHEMICALS

Pesticides, fungicides, growth promoters, colouring agents, stabilizers, flowing agents, preservatives, taste enhancers, etc, have only really entered our diet in the past few decades. They now pervade the food industry.

Fig. 5.1: Dietary changes over two million years

and nuts. These foods contain not glucose or sucrose but other 'sugars', such as fructose, maltose, galactose and arabinose, which the body has to convert before it can use. These natural sugars are absorbed from the intestine into the bloodstream, where they circulate and are converted into glycogen by the liver, then stored as glycogen in muscles and the liver itself. When the body needs sugar for muscular activity it produces adrenalin, which causes the glycogen to be converted rapidly into usable sugar in the form of glucose (see Figure 5.2).

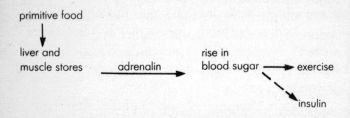

Fig. 5.2: Blood sugar responses in early humans

In our far distant ancestors, the only reasons for a rise in circulating blood sugar would have been because adrenalin was pumped out by the adrenal glands. This was always in response to some stimulus in the brain suggesting that exercise was likely to follow and that sugar was therefore needed to be made available immediately in order to make the muscles work efficiently. The stimuli behind this process could have been the sight of a marauding animal, suggesting the necessity of either running away or fighting it; a fight over property or a desired mate; or a hunt for food. Each stimulus, you will notice, involved a high degree of activity.

Nature, however, possibly with the twentieth century in mind, produced a back-up system to deal with the possibility that the rise in blood sugar might not be utilized in a fight or any other form of muscular activity. This was effected by insulin, one of whose chief functions is to bring a raised blood sugar level back to normal. What this means is that if muscular activity did not follow the rise in blood sugar (for example, the wild animal and hence the necessity to fight may have disappeared), insulin would have converted the blood sugar back into glycogen, ready for use another time.

Modern humans, on the other hand (see Figure 5.3) eat foods that are very high in sucrose (easily converted by the body into glucose without going

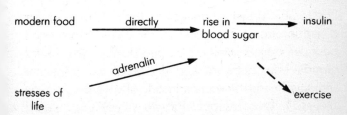

Fig. 5.3: Blood sugar responses in modern humans

through the glycogen-conversion process) and other refined carbohydrates, such as white flour, which the body treats in much the same way as sucrose. Many times in the day, then, there is a rise in blood sugar. Each cup of sweet tea or coffee, every sweet, chocolate, pudding, slice of white bread, or white flour product of any sort, causes a rise in blood sugar. But where is the exercise to reduce it? It may perhaps consist of a game of squash on Friday evening or a football match on Saturday afternoon, but will generally be many hours or days away from the regular rises in blood sugar that are taking place during the week. The insulin (supposedly back-up) system is called upon to act all the time.

Stresses of modern life, such as keeping up with the Joneses; arguments with the boss; worries over money, mortgage repayments or the children's schooling; ill-health; bereavement; or simply moving house – all these make the adrenalin pump out, which in turn causes a rise in blood sugar. It is seldom realized that alcohol, a cigarette (see Figure 5.4) or even a sugarless cup of coffee can lead to a rise in blood sugar.

Dr William Philpott in the USA is one of the clinical ecologists who have shown that a food or chemical allergic reaction nearly always also causes a rise in blood sugar. People today must spend much of their time with their blood sugar levels higher than they should be. Their insulin mechanism

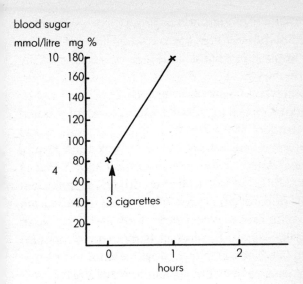

Fig. 5.4: Effect of cigarettes on the blood sugar level

is used far too often. It is not surprising that it becomes exhausted, leading to diabetes in some people or, at an earlier stage, causing others to manifest symptoms of hypoglycaemia, which for some unknown reason may persist for years without diabetes actually developing.

Tests for hypoglycaemia

There are two tests for hypoglycaemia which will go a long way to demonstrate that a person is not handling carbohydrates properly. The first is an extended glucose tolerance test (EGTT), the second is an insulin tolerance test (ITT).

The Extended Glucose Tolerance Test
This test is usually performed in a hospital laboratory, but could be done by a doctor or nurse in the surgery. The patient arrives at approximately 9am, having not had anything to eat or drink for 12 hours beforehand. On arrival, the patient should rest awhile and ideally should not have hurried to the laboratory or become flustered on the way there. Sometimes the patient is instructed to fill up with carbohydrate two or three days before the test, but that probably does not affect the result much.

A fasting sample of blood is taken, a 50g or 75g dose of glucose in any suitable form is swallowed and further blood samples are taken at half-hourly intervals for three hours, and then hourly, for a total of five hours. Four hours may perhaps be long enough, but the fifth hour sometimes shows results of value. This glucose load simulates a meal and shows how the person handles sugar.

Figure 5.5 shows what should be accepted as the normal range following the swallowing of a 50g glucose load. It will not be much different after a 75g dose. The specific features it demonstrates are the level of blood sugar in the fasting state and the gentle rise of sugar in the blood in the first hour,

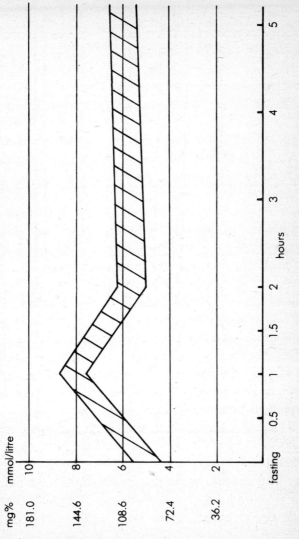

Fig. 5.5: Five-hour glucose tolerance test, 50g load – normal range

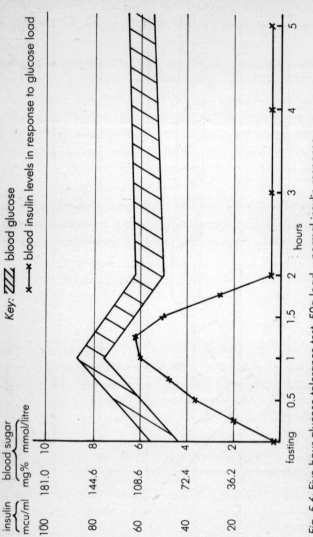

Fig. 5.6: Five-hour glucose tolerance test, 50g load – normal insulin response

Key: ▨▨ blood glucose
—×— blood insulin levels in response to glucose load

insulin mcu/ml	blood sugar mg%	mmol/litre
100	181.0	10
80	144.6	8
60	108.6	6
40	72.4	4
20	36.2	2

fasting 0.5 1 1.5 2 3 4 5
hours

reaching a level at least 50 per cent up from the fasting level but not going too high. This is then followed by a fall of blood sugar after all the sugar has been absorbed from the intestines. The fall should also be gentle and should not really fall below, or much below, the fasting level, reaching that level at about two hours. For the next three hours there should be very little change in the blood sugar levels if the person remains at rest.

Figure 5.6 shows the true normal range with levels of insulin marked as X. You will see there is a very low background level of insulin in the fasting stage, which rises gently to a maximum around 60mcu/ml, just after the peak of blood sugar has occurred. Insulin levels then fall, returning to their background level by the time the fasting level has been reached again, where it stays for the rest of the test.

Figure 5.7 shows what happens to a person's ability to handle a glucose load if he or she has spent a lifetime eating too much sugar and refined carbohydrate. Although the levels of blood sugar start off normal, the patient's absorptive mechanisms for sugar have been damaged and too much sugar has been absorbed too fast, leading to a level of blood sugar that is too high too soon. This takes the insulin mechanism by surprise (once again) and too much insulin is produced, the level reaching 90mcu/ml (again too early a rise and too high). As

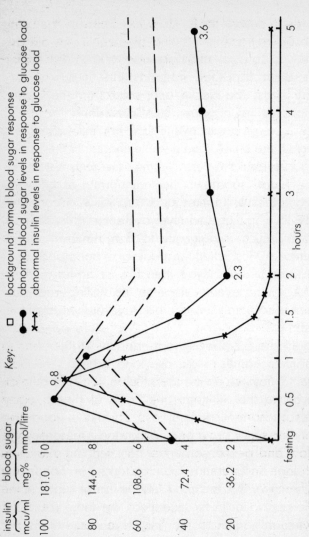

Fig. 5.7: Five-hour glucose tolerance test – abnormal result

Key:

□ background normal blood sugar response

● abnormal blood sugar levels in response to glucose load

✕ abnormal insulin levels in response to glucose load

a result, despite the fact that sugar may still be being absorbed from the intestine (although it may all have been absorbed in the first half-hour in some people), there is a rapid fall of blood sugar to dramatically low levels. The blood sugar value from the second to the fifth hour also remains below normal (certainly well under the fasting level) and insulin levels are still higher than they should be.

The patient is usually unaware of symptoms as the blood sugar is rising, certainly not before it reaches 10 or 12mmol/l. Symptoms will occur at the low level of 2.3 at two hours after the glucose load. What is very important to realize, however, is that symptoms occur if the *rate of fall* of the blood sugar is too fast. Although the level after an hour and a half (about 4.5mmol/l) might be considered quite reasonable, the blood sugar has fallen to that level from 9.8 in one hour. The body often responds to a rapid change in the blood sugar level rather than to the actual level.

It may help to consider the analogy of being on a plane that is coming in to land. If the plane descends very fast, you have difficulty in equalizing the pressure in your ears. If, however, the descent is slow and gentle, your ears can accommodate the change in pressure and you do not notice the difference. It is the same with levels of sugar in the blood. The faster the rate of fall, the more you suffer symptoms, even if the final level reached is not particularly low. The rate of the fall in blood sugar will be all the faster if it has shot up too quickly in the first place (see Figure 5.7) and if too much insulin has been produced as a consequence. Symptoms of hypoglycaemia can therefore occur either as a result of a particularly low level of sugar in the blood or as a result of a rapid fall from an abnormally high level.

If a patient complains of hypoglycaemic symptoms to his or her doctor, say about one and a half hours after a meal, the doctor may possibly arrange for a blood test at that time and find it to be 'normal', suggesting that the patient is imagining it all. Even if the doctor were to carry out an extended glucose tolerance test, a pattern similar to that in Figure 5.7 might be revealed, but the importance of the rate of fall of the blood sugar might not be recognized. Certainly patients can feel hungry and light-headed quite quickly after a meal or a sugary snack, and the reason should now be clear. The same person will, of course, have discovered that a sweet snack or sugary cup of tea or coffee can alleviate the symptoms and so, not surprisingly, he or she will continue to take such carbohydrate items whenever the symptoms seem to be coming on. This is a classic feature of the bingeing syndrome and may also apply to people experiencing withdrawal symptoms from smoking.

Patients may remain in the stage of reactivity, ie Stage 1, but if they move on to Stage 2 they may well think that the condition is correcting itself because they will then feel better for much of the time. Unfortunately, this is the calm before the storm of diabetes, as shown in Figure 5.8. The production of insulin has become rather sluggish in response to the rapid rise in blood sugar. You will note that the peak of the rise is higher and later than in Figure 5.7 but that the fall is slower and more gentle. Insulin is still being produced, but there is a tired response. The mechanism for insulin production is worn out by having been called upon so many times in the past. In fact, according to the criteria of the World Health Organization the patient shown in Figure 5.7 would be classified as diabetic already, as the two-hour blood sugar level is above 8mmol/l. I personally would say 'pre-diabetic', as the condition can be corrected at this stage. Sadly, it is unlikely that the condition will be recognized for what it is and so such a correction is unlikely to be made.

As the fall in blood sugar is slow and gentle, symptoms of hypoglycaemia can no longer be discerned from the rate of fall. Before the patient's blood sugar reaches 3.1 (at which level hypogly-caemic symptoms might occur, though not necessar-ily), he or she is likely to have the usual between-meals snacks, so pushing the level of blood sugar up again. Thus the regular attacks of hypoglycaemia that may have occurred in the past will seem to have disappeared and the patient may well be tempor-

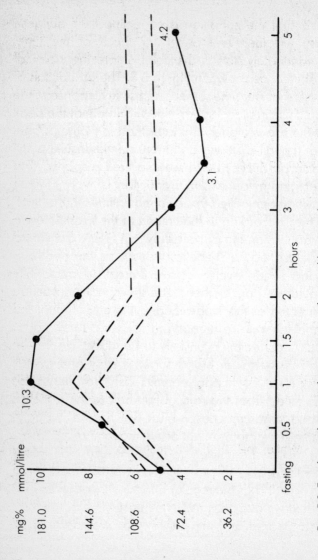

Fig. 5.8: Five-hour glucose tolerance test – abnormal later result

arily feeling better.

The next phase is the classic diabetic, whose profile is illustrated in Figure 5.9. A diabetic's level of blood sugar can sometimes rise astronomically. Figure 5.9 shows a rise to 13.2mmol/l, but patients in a diabetic (high blood sugar) coma can reach as high as 50mmol/l or more.

Insulin Tolerance Test

This test has to be carried out by a doctor, as it involves drawing a fasting blood sample for sugar analysis and then injecting insulin intravenously. Blood samples for sugar are usually drawn at intervals of 10, 20, 30, 45, 60, 90 and 120 minutes.

In healthy individuals, the 10, 20 and 30 minute samples should show a 50 per cent fall in blood sugar, rebounding to the fasting level at 120 minutes. If a patient has hypoglycaemia, cannot handle carbo-hydrate properly or has other mechanisms that are not working correctly, symptoms of hypoglycaemia will appear. Oral glucose should be available for immediate use if necessary, preferably after a blood sample has quickly been taken for sugar measurement. In extreme cases, intravenous glucose may be needed.

While this test demonstrates how the body responds to an intravenously administered dose of insulin and shows up any deficiencies in the mechanisms for countering low blood sugar, the five-hour glucose tolerance test is the more valuable, in my

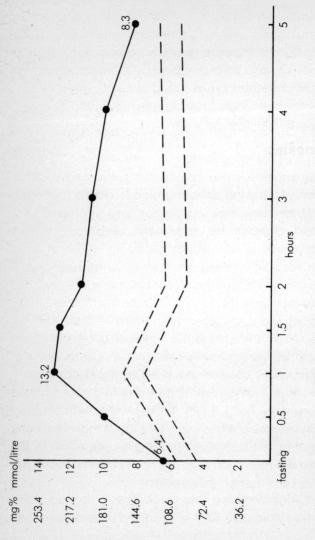

Fig. 5.9: Five-hour glucose tolerance test – diabetic curve

opinion, because it makes clear how the patient handles an oral glucose load. After all, it is the regular intake of sugar and refined carbohydrate over many years that has done the damage and that is what this test is simulating.

The importance of hypoglycaemia in smoking

You should now understand hypoglycaemia better than you did before you began to read this chapter and with any luck its relevance to your particular situation should now be clear. I hope you can now appreciate why symptoms sometimes occur, why you can feel unwell even after having eaten what appears to have been a satisfactory meal and why you can make yourself temporarily feel better by having more of such foods. The same mechanism is operating after you have smoked a cigarette and then, as your body experiences the sensations of withdrawal, you feel you need to smoke another.

If you understand this, it should make it all the more easy for you to realize why you must stop eating some of those particular foods that are clearly causing rebound hypoglycaemia and which in the long run make you crave all sorts of items, including, to a certain extent, cigarettes.

A person's life history is likely to reveal episodes of hypoglycaemia if it is examined in enough detail.

If it does, a full analysis of that person's diet, both present and past, will reveal a high intake of sugar, refined carbohydrate, coffee and other equally addictive foods or drinks. This information will make it easier to explain any current symptoms and to prescribe suitable treatment, for instance to tell the patient to avoid sugar. Remember, quite apart from the effects of their smoking, most smokers have problems or complaints that could be caused by other factors.

Lifestyle and health

People often notice things about themselves, how they react to certain situations and what makes them feel unwell or better, but rarely analyse their observations in order to help themselves get better. In my practice I apply the approach of medical detective, ask many questions and then try to interpret the information in such a way as to be helpful to the patient. Much of the time tests are not needed, for a good observer and interpreter of those observations will be able to make recommendations which nearly always lead to the patient feeling better.

To digress awhile, I have seen over 1,000 patients suffering from multiple sclerosis (MS). On the form which I ask them to fill in before they come to see me, three or four have indicated that they smoked about four cigarettes a day. Much to their surprise, my reaction to that was not: 'Why do you smoke?', but: 'Why do you smoke so few?' In every case the answer has been along the lines of, 'I like to smoke, but when I do it gives me pins and needles in my fingers or toes, so I keep the number down.'

What these patients were saying, in fact, was that smoking could actually produce symptoms of their MS. It had never occurred to them that if they stopped smoking it might help their symptoms to go. No-one had ever suggested to them that smoking could have anything to do with multiple sclerosis, because doctors are not taught the possibility of such a link. Yet here were patients clearly identifying smoking as something that could provoke MS symptoms in them.

To take this a step further, I usually find that these patients had already discovered that their symptoms could be exacerbated if they ate tomatoes, which they did avoid, and that they might be 'addicted' to potatoes, perhaps eating them with every meal as well as snacking on crisps in between. There was generally a great sense of alarm when I suggested that they should stop eating potatoes altogether. Yet potatoes, tomatoes, aubergines (or eggplant), peppers and tobacco are all part of the deadly nightshade family in the biological classification of plants. As cross-reactions within the food family can sometimes occur, giving up all these foods often helps the complaint or reaction to go.

Knowledge of a person's lifestyle and history is essential to making this kind of judgement.

I treat people with many different ailments and symptoms which usually respond very well to the patient making a change in their lifestyle such as altering his or her diet. Multiple sclerosis, arthritis, hyperactivity in children, eczema, irritable bowel syndrome, depression or simply a wide variety of symptoms that do not add up to one known problem can all respond to this approach. I explain things fully to people and offer them an alternative to drugs, but my treatment always involves them doing something for themselves.

Most people's histories give clues as to why they are ill, if those clues can be found and then interpreted. I work on the simple assumption that any organ that is producing symptoms is being irritated or inflamed by something. If you smoke and have a cough, it is reasonable to assume that the cigarette smoke is irritating your lungs. If you have a blister on your foot, it is reasonable to assume that the skin of your foot is being irritated by the material of your shoe. I simply ask the question: what is irritating the joint of a person suffering from arthritis, the nervous tissue of a person suffering from MS or the lungs of a person suffering from bronchitis? In fact this approach can be applied to any symptom or ailment.

The question is easy to ask. It is not always so

easy to find the answer, but then you will never look for the answer, let alone find it, if you do not ask the question. This approach appears so simple and basic to me that I cannot understand why it is not more generally accepted.

After all, if you suffer from arthritis and you visit your doctor, after appropriate examinations and possibly some tests, you will probably be prescribed an anti-inflammatory drug. If you ask how it works, the answer may perhaps be that when you swallow the drug it is absorbed from the intestines into the bloodstream, where it circulates and ends up at the joints. In the joints it acts to cool the inflammation and so, it is hoped, helps you to feel better. Yet the inflammation may have been caused in the first place by something entering the body in the same way as the cure, via the mouth, that is to say as a result of what you have been eating or drinking. It too may have been absorbed into the bloodstream and circulated round to the joints, where it caused the inflammation of arthritis. Had it caused an inflammation in the skin you would have had dermatitis or eczema, if in the nervous tissue maybe it would have resulted in multiple sclerosis.

If that sounds far-fetched, remember that it is totally accepted that alcohol (taken in through the mouth) can cause light-headedness and various other effects, down to drunkenness and uncon-sciousness. The reactions can be greater in some people than in others. Similarly peanuts, shellfish and other foods can cause swelling of the lips and larynx and breathing problems such as asthma. Strawberries can lead to skin rashes. Migraines are commonly an allergic reaction to cheese, chocolate and red wine. A considerable amount of such evidence is accepted by the orthodox medical profession, but its members are still generally reluctant to consider the possibility that other things taken by mouth may cause symptoms in any part of the body, albeit not in such a clear-cut and obvious way.

Personally, I see no reason why all symptoms and so-called diseases cannot be explained in this way. If you accept this possibility, then you must accept the possibility that things may enter the body in other ways to cause inflammation. Thus maybe the lungs or skin can be further points of entry for some 'inflammatory' substances.

If you sit in a traffic jam for too long, you can develop a headache. Presumably the traffic fumes are absorbed via the lungs to affect your brain. A general anaesthetic given through a face mask enters the bloodstream via the lungs to put you to sleep. The same effect, however, can be achieved by putting an anaesthetic directly into a vein. A person particularly sensitive to aspirin might have an asthmatic attack when such a tablet is taken for a headache. Nerve gas is absorbed via the skin.

What I am really trying to say is that when faced

with a range of complaints or symptoms, orthodox medicine assumes that the body has simply gone wrong and has to be corrected either by cutting the problem out (for example the appendix), or by giving the person a medicine or drug which in fact only suppresses the symptoms (if you stop the drug the symptoms come back again). This may help the person to feel better (which is certainly important), but does not attack the basic cause of the problem. If this can be found and eliminated, the symptoms will not only go, but will stay away because the root cause has been dealt with. Moreover, the patient will no longer need to carry on taking drugs.

I do not wish to be critical of what doctors are taught in medical school, because applying the methods taught there has helped countless numbers of people and saved many from death, so clearly they are effective. I just wish that orthodox medicine would not consider them to be the only methods available and would realize that the approach I have described also has a most important place in medicine today.

Lifestyle and diagnosis

The effectiveness of this approach can be illustrated by a case study from my practice. The patient in question was in her late thirties when I first saw her and was brought to me by her husband because she suffered from a condition called Friedrich's Ataxia, a nasty hereditary form of multiple sclerosis. Her condition was pretty desperate. Whenever she tried to do anything with her arms, she would shake violently, rather like the intention tremor of a patient suffering from Parkinsonism. In her case, however, the shaking was very coarse and violent, so it was dangerous for her to try to feed herself as she might have stabbed herself in the face, although more likely the food would shake off the fork. In any case, she could not pick up the instruments as her control of her fingers was so poor.

The woman was also partially blind and her speaking was totally unintelligible to me, although her husband could understand her some of the time. She was totally paralysed from the waist downwards, completely unable to move any part of her legs. Her brother had died of the same condition when he was three years younger than she was now. She knew she was dying and would die soon and was, not surprisingly, very depressed. When she came to see me the first time, although she listened to every word I said, she never smiled. I doubt if she expected me to be able to help. After all, she had seen many experts and no-one had offered her any chance at all.

I went into her history very carefully, noting certain items which indicated something to me. At each stage I told her what I was thinking of, but I could understand if, at this point, she could not really see why it would help her.

There is a place on the form I send to people in advance of their coming to see me that asks them to list anything at all that they know can influence their symptoms, either for better or for worse, or in any way affect them. These aspects of a person's history are of extreme importance. They are not just clues; if interpreted properly they can be the source of information that can be used most successfully to help patients get better. This patient, through her husband, told me a most fascinating fact.

In addition to all the problems I have already outlined, she suffered from quite bad headaches two or three times most weeks. She had noticed on more than one occasion that if she took aspirin for her headache it would clear the pain, but would also have a devastating effect upon her shakes. Under normal circumstances the tremors were only bad if she tried to move her arms purposefully, which at the best of times was difficult anyway. If she kept still she did not seem to shake. Taking aspirin, however, would make her condition appallingly worse even when she was at rest, to such an extent that she would shake from head to toe like a really cold person, except that this would go on for three or four days, gradually settling down until she returned to the pattern of shaking only if she tried to do anything. While she was reacting to the aspirin she simply could not sleep and ended up totally exhausted.

Not surprisingly, my patient seldom ever took aspirin because of its devastating effect upon her and she might well not have mentioned it to me if the symptoms had not been so very severe. She had told many doctors about this in the past and her notes had 'allergic to aspirin' stamped in red letters all over them, even though this is a most unusual reaction and not a typical allergic one at all. As might be expected, she had been advised many times to avoid aspirin – but that is all.

When I said to her, 'Has no one ever told you that 25 per cent of the foods you are eating at present contain a natural form of aspirin called salicylate?' a vestige of a smile crossed her face for the first time. She began to see at last what I was getting at, why I was digging into her history so deeply.

There is no test I know of that can check if a person is allergic to salicylates, but I did not need one. My patient effectively told me that aspirin (salicylates) could make her shake. Her history was therefore demanding that she try the effect of a salicylate-free diet.

Now you may think I had found something extraordinary, but I hadn't. She had told many doctors of the effect aspirin had upon her, but their orthodox approach did not allow them to take that part of her history to its logical conclusion. Yet skin specialists know that a salicylate-free diet may be worth tying in some people who complain of hives, urticaria or a nettle-rash skin irritation. Ear, nose and throat specialists are aware that nasal polyps may respond to a salicylate-free diet, even though they seldom try it ('Diets are so difficult, aren't they?' they often say) and don't even tell their patients that there is such an alternative, merely explaining to them that they can operate to remove the polyps each time they grow back.

Some hyperactive children and some people with asthma respond to a salicylate-free diet. All hospital dieticians are trained to explain such a diet to any patient whose doctor thinks it is worth trying. So why didn't anyone suggest it to this patient?

Further aspects of my patient's history suggested one or two other things worth trying, which by now she was quite willing to do as she saw the excitement in my face at picking up such an obvious clue. When I saw her four weeks later I did not recognize her – she had an enormous smile on her face. Within four days of starting the diet I had recommended, her tremors had started to clear and a week or so later she was feeding herself and was completely free from the shaking. Although her condition had other effects on her arms, weakening them and reducing her dexterity, she could now manage to feed herself – with obvious delight at her new-found freedom.

The woman's vision had improved 50 per cent, even though her voice was still unintelligible to me. She could also now stand out of her wheelchair and take simple pleasure in putting weight on her own legs, helped by her husband at this stage. As time has gone by all of these symptoms have improved and when I last saw her I could understand every word she said. All of us tend naturally to be optimistic for the future, but this woman knows that she is going to progress and gradually get better and, more importantly, that she is not going to die from this condition at a young age. I hope for a total recovery eventually, but I have not promised it.

This is a graphic example of how a patient's history can be informative, to such an extent that if interpreted properly it can point the way to alleviating symptoms and even to overcoming them completely some time in the future, whatever they are. A course of action was so obvious to me when I heard this woman's story, and so apparently effective when it was tried, that I wonder why her previous doctors had not followed the same clues.

This is the point that I want to make — how simple my approach can be. Most patient's histories give me useful clues and I explain as much as possible to them in the time we have available, so that they know what they are being asked to do and why. That is what this book is all about. With any luck you will see the basic common sense behind it and feel it is worthwhile applying this advice to giving up smoking.

Smoking can cause hypoglycaemia

The case study above hightlighted the importance of knowing about a person's history and lifestyle before prescribing a course of treatment. This knowledge is also fundamental in judging the effects of smoking, particularly because cigarette smoke may interact with other factors.

Although most people accept that withdrawal symptoms occur when a smoker stops smoking, it is assumed that these effects are caused only by the withdrawal of nicotine. In fact an experiment I once carried out on a patient showed that the withdrawal symptoms may be produced in part by rebound low blood sugar, and that the effects of low levels of nicotine in the blood may be exaggerated by the low levels of sugar in the blood, or possibly by the change in blood sugar.

I once had a patient who was a hospital laboratory worker and came to me complaining of a variety of symptoms. She explained that she often felt generally unwell, light-headed, a bit queasy, slightly sweaty and hungry and she also had palpitations, especially early in the afternoon. It did not seem to be too relevant whether or not she had

had lunch. This was her main complaint, but the same symptoms could also occur at other times of the day, which she had not really been able to identify properly.

Like many places of work, the laboratory where my patient worked was very busy and she was not always able to take off enough time for lunch. If there was something that needed to be done urgently, she would simply do it without complaining, knowing that it could be extremely important for some patient in the hospital. She would, however, usually manage to find the time to have a cigarette while she was waiting for a reaction to take place in the test she had been asked to do. She would go to the smoking room and would sometimes, but by no means always, make herself a cup of coffee or tea to accompany the cigarette.

About an hour later, she would start to feel odd and the typical features of low blood sugar would develop. She could cope with them, however, and they would go if she had a snack or another drink. In her favour, she tried not to smoke too often during the day, so she may not have been too addicted.

The woman was aware that her hypoglycaemic symptoms could be made worse, but not always, if she had had a cup of tea or coffee with her cigarette, or if she had had a meal. But she could not understand it because she felt that what she usually ate at lunchtimes should have kept her going for the rest of the day. Rebound hypoglycaemia had never been explained to her. I felt that her story indicated that smoking caused hypoglycaemia, as her infrequent cigarettes suggested that she was not badly addicted to nicotine. She did not really want to give up her few cigarettes a day, however, as she thought she enjoyed them. She made the usual excuses that a cigarette helped her to relax during the day, or was part of her normal routine after a meal, plus all the other reasons people give when they try to fool themselves into not giving up.

I therefore suggested that we try an experiment to see if we could demonstrate the harm that smoking did to her by looking at the possible effect of cigarettes on her blood sugar. I explained that it might be necessary to reinforce the effect in order to demonstrate the point more forcefully. As she was smoking every day, it might be difficult to know what her real blood sugar level was. So it might be better for her to give up smoking for a few days to allow her blood sugar levels to settle, if smoking were somehow upsetting them, and then challenge her with two or three cigarettes. In the end this is what we did.

On an agreed day my patient stopped smoking and stayed off cigarettes for five days. On the morning of the sixth day she went into work without having had anything to eat or drink since the previous midnight, exactly the same conditions as would be applied to a glucose tolerance test. She was asked to take her time, not to hurry and to try to arrive at work in a calm state. She was advised to warn her friends and colleagues of what she was going to do in case withdrawal symptoms did make her a bit ill-tempered. She of course asked someone to take blood samples from her.

When she arrived, she settled down in the laboratory. Her colleague took a sample of blood from a vein in the normal hospital way, in order to measure her blood sugar level in the fasting state. The woman then smoked three cigarettes one after the other, inhaling the smoke in her normal way and taking as long as usual over each cigarette.

She timed when she started smoking and when she finished and worked out the middle point, which we designated her 'smoking time'. Every quarter of an hour from then on (as she worked in a laboratory we were able to do the blood tests more often than usual), her colleague took a sample of blood for blood sugar measurements, just as in a glucose tolerance test, except of course that she had not had a dose of sugar but simply the three cigarettes one after the other. She did not have any more cigarettes or anything to eat or drink until the experiment was finished.

The result of this smoking-blood sugar test is shown in Figure 5.10. If you compare it to Figure 5.4 on page 71 you will see that her blood sugar shot up high within one hour, presumably producing a rapid rise in insulin. This was then followed by not

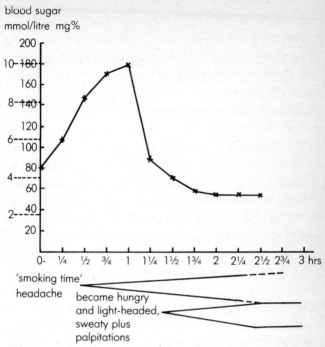

Fig. 5.10: Smoking challenge test on smoker after avoiding cigarettes for five days – the effect on her blood sugar

only a rapid fall in blood sugar (remember I explained that the *rate* of change may be more important than the actual level itself), but also a fall to a sufficiently low level to produce hypoglycaemic symptoms.

As Figure 5.10 shows, the patient began to develop a headache after about 20 minutes, which gradually got worse as time went by. In addition she became light-headed and hungry at about one hour 20 minutes; together with other symptoms, such as palpitations, sweating and generally feeling really quite unwell, this gradually became worse, probably peaking after about two and a half hours. By this time she was lying down in a darkened room 'wanting to die'.

Once the blood test results were to hand, her colleague rang me with them and I agreed there was no need to continue with the experiment. I suggested the technician have something sweet to bring her blood sugar level up and even suggested she could have a cigarette. Interestingly enough, she refused as she said she had learned her lesson.

When I saw my patient two weeks later, she was feeling enormously better and had not smoked a single cigarette since our 'experiment' and felt she really did not want one. The test had opened her eyes to the profound effect smoking had on her blood sugar levels. It explained to her in a thoroughly scientific way (remember where she worked) what her symptoms had been saying to her all along, but which she had attempted to ignore in the hope that they would go away eventually.

All too often smokers seem to need some sort of 'demonstration' that smoking is doing them harm. They go on fooling themselves that they are 'enjoying their smoking' and keep making the usual futile excuses. I know of absolutely no evidence that smoking is of any benefit whatsoever to anyone. The so-called tension-relief or relaxation from stress that some smokers insist is why they continue to smoke, is simply experienced because their whole bodies are in an addicted state and when they smoke they are relieving withdrawal symptoms from the previous cigarette.

Alternatively, a cigarette may be one way in which a smoker can elevate his or her blood sugar level, which is depressed in the first instance either by the last cigarette that was smoked, or by low blood sugar rebound an hour or so after taking something else that caused the blood sugar to rise high, such as a cup of coffee or anything unnecessarily sweet. At this stage it could well be worthwhile re-reading the earlier part of this chapter, where hypoglycaemia is fully described, as it is such a simple explanation of what so many people feel periodically, not just those who smoke.

The phenomenon of rebound low blood sugar is often denied by doctors because they were not taught it in medical school, nor did they have it explained to them in their post-graduate sessions. The examples of glucose tolerance tests given above are from real people, so the scientific laboratory results can hardly be questioned. What is difficult for many doctors to understand is that symptoms can occur at a seemingly acceptable level of blood sugar if it has fallen from a considerable height. As I keep stressing, it is the rate of fall of blood sugar that can often produce hypoglycaemic symptoms. (It is worth noting that a rapid *fall* in blood sugar produces unpleasant symptoms, whereas a rapid *rise* has no obvious effect, just as making a steep climb in an aeroplane has little effect on one's ears, in contrast to a fast or even normal descent in a plane.)

Avoidance and challenge

When I described the method of testing I wanted the smoking lab technician to adopt, I explained to her that we might need to reinforce the effect that smoking had on her in order to demonstrate the point more forcefully. As she was smoking every day, I suggested it might be difficult to know what her real blood sugar level was, so it might be better for her to give up smoking for a few days and allow her blood sugar to reach its own level in case smoking was somehow affecting it. She therefore agreed to give up cigarettes for five days and then to smoke three cigarettes one after the other.

Although the reason I gave was quite genuine and I thought it would make for a better test, I did also have an ulterior motive. I have been practising this kind of medical detective work for nearly 20 years. Like all learning processes, you need to start simply. One way of identifying food reactions is called 'avoidance and challenge'.

In Chapter 3 I described the basic principles of

addiction and showed how Professor Hans Selyé managed to demonstrate the three stages that the body goes through when challenged regularly by something potentially harmful. In Stage 1 the reaction is obvious, ie a reaction takes place, even though where humans are concerned it is not always obvious what has actually caused the reaction, or even that the reaction is a reaction to anything in particular.

For example, to most people, and indeed to most doctors, a headache is just a headache. If asked for the cause, 'tension' is likely to be the answer, ie a fob-off or an implied: 'it's your fault'. The headache was in fact probably a result of a cup of coffee, red wine, chocolate or something similar, but its cause is likely to be ignored. After all, don't a great many people have a great many headaches? Yes, they do, but they don't need to!

In Stage 2, because the body is adapting to the substance (it may be able to continue adapting for a very long time, or may eventually give up the effort when the adaptive mechanisms have become exhausted, which is when Stage 3 begins), there may be very few symptoms of any significance. Indeed there may be a slight general lift, with the occasional low episode which is simply shrugged off as 'just one of those things', or 'I must have been overdoing things'.

In Stage 3, the stage when addiction has really started to become a problem, symptoms of any sort (such as headaches, aches and pains, low blood sugar symptoms or just feeling under the weather) occur when the addictive substance is stopped or given up, even for only a few hours. That is why many people *need* a cup of tea or coffee to start the day, having not had a dose for the hours when they were asleep, ie since their last cup before going to bed. Others *need* a bar of chocolate every so often. The addict's body somehow feels let down without its regular dose, its regular fix.

I tend to see people when they have already entered Stage 3, or have been in it for some time. At their first visit they say they have had their symtoms for months or years, or they may not even be able to remember when they last felt at all well. Some of my patients have been ill all their lives, probably from birth or even in the womb, having given their mothers a very hard time during pregnancy.

There are many things that can make people ill but, despite much excellent evidence published by some of the world's top medical professors and doctors, the idea that what people eat and drink may be the underlying cause of their ill-health has not really permeated to the thinking and teaching of most of the medical profession as yet.

When the food reaction is obvious, no-one doubts it has occurred. Typical examples are a rash that develops after eating strawberries, swelling of the lips caused by peanuts or diarrhoea after having fish.. Remember, these are accepted food allergies which occur in specifically susceptible people. Only a minority of people react to these foods; the majority are totally unaffected when they eat them. When the reactions occur, they do so soon after the person has consumed the allergen, which is a food that the person has not been eating on a regular basis. In other words, they were an unusual food for that person, so that when a reaction did take place he or she had no difficulty in identifying the cause.

'Oh, I know! I ate those strawberries for tea. That's what's caused this rash.'

The reaction to foodstuffs that I am talking about, however, is not such an obvious one and does not occur every time that the particular food is eaten. Indeed, the food to which a person is eventually found to have been reacting is often one commonly eaten that seems to produce less obvious, but probably more drawn-out reactions. These are reactions that are not normally associated with foods by most doctors, such as a blocked nose or an inflamed joint.

There are many ways of identifying which foods are the cause of a person's ill-health and one of the simplest is the avoidance-and-challenge test. This is exactly what it says. The person must for a time avoid whatever food is suspected of producing the reaction and then eat it again as a challenge, to see if it provokes symptoms.

Because many foods may be involved in a

particular person's symptoms, or certainly more than one (but you don't know which ones, or you wouldn't be doing the test), it may be best to avoid all foods and drinks for the period of avoidance, which means a total fast drinking bottled spring water only.

I do not intend to discuss the avoidance-and-challenge system here in any detail, because when I last taught it to doctors, in order for them to understand it well enough to take patients safely through it, it took me three hours to cover what they needed to know. I have, however, covered it in enough detail, in my earlier book, *Conquering Cystitis*,* for people to take themselves through it in safety. I would certainly not advise anyone to do the avoidance-and-challenge test for foods without either being supervised by a doctor competent in the method or reading my book first.

All I will say here is that a five-day avoidance period has been found from experience to be the ideal length of time, so that challenge feeding can begin on the morning of Day 6. A list of foods needs to have been drawn up in advance and on the sixth day the person can then start to eat these one by one. If a food that is subsequently identified as being one of the culprits is by chance introduced as the

*Published by ABACO Publishing, 72 Main Street, Osgathorpe, Leics LE12 9TA. Price £6.95 plus post and packaging: £1 in the UK, £3 outside the UK.

tenth food, or later, the reaction to eating it will not be too bad because it will be some days after the food has been introduced before the first reaction occurs. If, on the other hand, one of the foods that are causing the problem is the very first food introduced, the reaction will be at its greatest. It has been found from experience that for most people avoidance of the food for five days, followed by its challenge on the sixth day, will produce a far more severe reaction than if it were introduced on Day 4 after only three days of avoidance, or on Day 10, however long the period of total avoidance.

Perhaps now you can see why I was rather sneaky in suggesting to my lab technician that she give up cigarettes for five days (supposedly to clear the effect of nicotine from her body and to let her blood sugar settle to a non-smoking level) and then do the three-cigarette challenge on the morning of Day 6. (I did subsequently explain what I had done to her once she had given up smoking.) As I was sure from her history that cigarette-smoking was a principal cause of her symptoms, I wanted to achieve the maximum effect possible from the test. I wanted the cigarettes after five days of avoidance to make her feel really ill and to have a clear effect upon her blood sugar. As far as I am concerned the test was a great success. More to the point, however, it showed me one way of helping people to give up smoking.

6

How craving works

Now that you have read all about how addictions occur to a range of substances, not only to tobacco but also to sugar, coffee, alcohol, tea and cheese, to name some of the more common ones, and you can see how hypoglycaemia fits into the whole pattern, the relevance of this information to giving up smoking should become clearer.

Figure 6.1 shows my idea of what happens to your blood nicotine levels when you smoke normally. The horizontal line is what I call the 'craving line', somewhere below which a sense of craving develops. The craving line is a product of my imagination, but to all intents and purposes it signifies a level of nicotine in the blood, anywhere below which you start to crave a cigarette. Anywhere above it you do not crave a cigarette. You can go a long way above, but naturally you do your general health a lot of harm in the process. This is very similar to levels of blood sugar that rise too high.

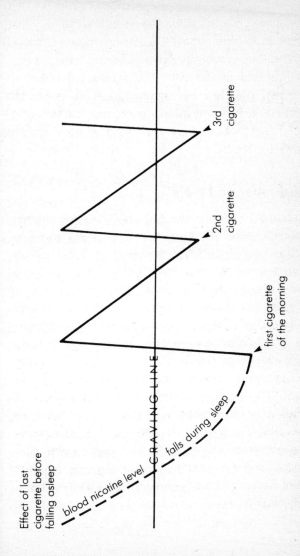

Fig. 6.1: The effect on levels of blood nicotine when smoking 'normally'

Effect of last cigarette before falling asleep

blood nicotine level

CRAVING LINE

falls during sleep

first cigarette of the morning

2nd cigarette

3rd cigarette

Despite the arbitrary nature of the craving line, it helps to explain what is going on in your body at any one time. From my observations of people and life in general, I believe the craving line can move up or down, affected by circumstances such as the mood you are in, any infection you may be suffering, or anything that can take your mind off how you are feeling.

Blood nicotine levels

In Figure 6.1 you presumably smoke a cigarette at a particular time, say your first one in the morning, because you crave it. You therefore start the morning below the craving line. During the night your blood level of nicotine has fallen and most people are not awoken by an awareness of craving. If they do wake in the middle of the night, they may well sit up and light a cigarette, going comfortably back to sleep again when they have finished.

The fact that you cannot smoke while you are asleep shows either that the setting of the craving line alters, or that there is a system that effectively blocks the symptoms of withdrawal and therefore ignores the craving line. Quite clearly the level of nicotine in the blood falls after the last cigarette of the evening. If a person smokes 20 cigarettes a day, he or she must be smoking more than one cigarette an hour and there may be a concentration of cigarette-smoking in the so-called relaxed atmosphere of the evening or around mealtimes.

Assuming that most cigarettes are smoked because of a sense of craving (although they are often smoked simply out of habit or because someone offers you one), then presumably the blood nicotine level will fall below the craving line about an hour or so after the last cigarette. There is no reason to believe that the pattern of this fall in blood nicotine is any different at night than during the daytime. Consequently, when you smoke your last cigarette at night before going to bed, your blood nicotine levels presumably rise and fall as they always do, ie. following the pattern of Figure 6.1. What I am saying is that within an hour or so of the last cigarette of the day, you would be craving another cigarette if you were awake. If you have fallen asleep, your craving is not sufficiently strong to wake you. The fact that you are asleep prevents you from responding to the low level of blood nicotine.

When you wake up your blood nicotine level will be even lower than in the early hours of the morning, as it will fall further the longer you go without a cigarette. As I explained in relation to a fall of blood sugar producing hypoglycaemic symptoms, most people suffer from hypoglycaemia because of a rapid fall in their blood sugar levels, and the actual level itself may not be particularly low. However, at a certain low level, irrespective of how long it has taken to fall to that level, symptoms of hypoglycaemia will eventually appear.

Similarly, during the night your blood nicotine levels will fall further and further so that when you wake up the level will almost undoubtedly be low enough to inspire a sense of craving. Hence you light up, bringing your blood nicotine level back up above the craving line and you feel relieved.

In general, then, a regular smoker will follow the pattern of Figure 6.1. The first cigarette of the day relieves the craving symptoms produced by a fall in blood nicotine during the night, as the craving line is crossed. Maximum levels of blood nicotine are reached by the end of smoking a cigarette, as all the nicotine that is to be absorbed into the bloodstream is absorbed immediately by inhalation via the lungs. Nicotine does not remain in your lungs to be released some minutes later and push your blood nicotine up slowly.

The lungs are an extremely efficient way of getting something into the bloodstream. They are as efficient as an intravenous injection. This is in contrast to taking something by mouth. If you swallow a tablet on an empty stomach, first it has to dissolve in the stomach, then pass into the duodenum and be absorbed in the jejunum, which means that it does not reach its maximum level in the bloodstream for at least half an hour and usually longer. If absorption is delayed by taking the drug with food, the peak blood level will be later still and will also probably not be as high.

Cigarette smoke, however, can be handled by your lungs just like the oxygen you breathe in and the carbon dioxide you breathe out all the time. The maximum blood level of nicotine is reached by the end of the cigarette, after which the level starts to fall towards the craving line. Symptoms of craving begin when it crosses that line, depending upon either the rate by which it has fallen, or the depth to which it has actually fallen.

When you read Chapter 8, you will realize how relevant this chapter is, because there you will find how to control the level of nicotine in your blood deliberately. You will be asked to be conscious of where your craving line is, how you feel and what you must do to cope with the situation. It will not be at all difficult, because my instructions are quite simple. You will also be armed with the understanding of what is actually happening inside your body. Knowledge gives you control. If you understand what you are doing, you will do it all the more easily. Giving up smoking will be easy.

7

Food addictions and smoking

Now we come to the 'real' chapters of this book – the ones where I describe what you do to give up smoking. I hope by now you have understood all that has gone before, that it makes sense to you. I spend a good deal of time explaining to my patients why they are ill, what has gone wrong and what we can do to put things right. If you do not know the cause of the problem, you cannot easily correct it. In terms of ill-health, all that most doctors can do is cut out the offending organ or give you a drug to suppress the symptoms. That may make you feel better, but it will not have resolved the basic problem at all. I do not object to symptom relief – it is certainly essential and good medicine in its way. But for many people it is unsatisfactory, some find it just does not work and the poor unfortunate few have an adverse reaction to the drugs the doctor tries. In any case, for a number of conditions there is no treatment that can be tried.

Remember how I described addictions in detail in Chapter 3? The vast majority (probably all) of those who find it difficult to give up smoking are addicted to nicotine. Anyone who is addicted to nicotine and cannot give up reasonably easily is in an addictive state, a problem which must be attended to.

Remember how I said I do not know how anyone succeeds in drying out from alcohol in a special unit when they are allowed free access to equally potentially addictive substances such as cigarettes, coffee and sugar? These too need to be attended to at the same time.

If you are addicted to coffee but give it up, you will undoubtedly suffer from withdrawal symptoms for the first few days. You are likely to suffer in the same way if you give up any addictive substance. However, if you give up more than one substance to which you are addicted, the withdrawal symptoms you suffer will be no more severe than if you had only given up the worst offender on its own. So you might as well give up all addictive substances at the same time. In fact it may be best if you give up your other addictions for a week before starting to give up cigarettes.

How do you identify your addictions? First of all, be aware that the most commonly addictive sub-stances that people regularly take into their bodies are sugar, coffee, tea, cheese and chocolate. There are occasionally others, but these are the usual ones. This list has not included alcohol, which everyone knows is possibly addictive. The foods and drinks I have just mentioned are rarely thought of as addictive substances, so consider them carefully.

Keeping an inventory of your diet

Perhaps the best thing to do first is to draw up a four-day inventory of your diet. This means writing down everything you eat, drink or put into your mouth for four consecutive days. Carry paper and pencil around with you and write down things as you eat them. This is very important; if you do it later you are bound to forget something. Compile your inventory over a weekend, ie Friday, Saturday, Sunday, Monday, as you will therefore cover two weekdays (presumably workdays) and two weekend days, although I appreciate that may not apply to every-one.

It does not matter what form the inventory takes. It could be like the list of a chef preparing a menu of what is to be eaten over the next few days, and it should be in amazing detail. Table 7.1 gives such a chart and is adapted from the chart of one particular patient, with details added from others to show how complete it should be. The four days of the inventory should be reasonably typical of your regular habits.

When I ask a person to do a four-day inventory,

Table 7.1: Four-day dietary inventory

	Friday 6th Dec	Saturday 7th Dec	Sunday 8th Dec	Monday 9th Dec
Early	0700 hrs. Mug of tea with milk.	0730–0930 hrs. 2 mugs of tea with milk.	0800–0930 hrs. 2 mugs of tea with milk.	0645 hrs. Mug of tea with milk.
Breakfast	0700 hrs. Cereal – Cornflakes, Harvest Crunch with milk and a sprinkle of demerara sugar. Fried egg on fried brown bread (cooked in vegetable oil). One mug instant coffee with cream and two teaspoonfuls of white sugar. Toast, light textured brown, scrape of butter and marmalade.	1000 hrs. 2 rashers of grilled bacon, 2 grilled tomatoes, 2 slices of potato sautéed in vegetable oil. 2½ slices of toasted white bread, scrape of butter on each, honey. 2 mugs of ground coffee with cream and 2 teaspoonfuls demerara sugar. 1230 hrs. 1 pint bitter, packet of plain crisps and a Mars Bar.	1000 hrs. Cereal – Cornflakes, Grape Nuts, top of the milk, sprinkle of demerara sugar. 1 large boiled egg. 2 large slices of wholemeal toast, scrape of butter, honey. 2 mugs of freshly ground coffee, each with cream and 2 teaspoonfuls demerara sugar.	0745 hrs. Cereal – Cornflakes with Harvest Crunch, sprinkle of demerara sugar and top of the milk. 1 rasher of bacon, grilled tomato, 1½ large slices of wholemeal toast, scrape of butter, marmalade. 1100 hrs. Mug of instant coffee, cream and 2 white sugars. 2 chocolate digestive biscuits.

117

Table 7.1 continued

	Friday 6th Dec	Saturday 7th Dec	Sunday 8th Dec	Monday 9th Dec
Lunch	1315 hrs. Grilled smoked mackerel, squeeze of lemon, cauliflower, ½ pint cider, 1 Kit-Kat. 2 pieces of chewing gum.	1500 hrs. Grilled ham and cheese on toast (white bread). 1 banana. Thin slice of melon.	1245 hrs. 1 mug instant coffee, cream and 2 white sugars. 1330 hrs. 6 oz lentil and vegetable soup (home-made). 2 small slices white toast with cheese. 2 small mince pies with single cream.	1300 hrs. Fried whitebait (in corn oil), squeeze of lemon, tinned carrots, ½ pint of cider, packet of salt-and-vinegar crisps. 1 Kit-Kat.
pm	1515 hrs. Mug of instant coffee, 'Coffee Plus', 2 teaspoonfuls of white sugar.		1600 hrs. Mug of instant coffee with cream and 2 teaspoonfuls of demerara sugar. 4 oz bar Cadbury's Milk Chocolate.	15.30 hrs. Cup of instant coffee with cream and 2 white sugars.
Tea	1730 hrs. 2 mugs of tea with milk. Slice of currant cake.	1730 hrs. 2 mugs of tea with milk. Small currant sponge. 1 cup cake. Small piece of chocolate sponge.	1820 hrs. Mug of tea with milk. Small currant sponge cup cake.	1730 hrs. Mug of tea with milk. Small piece of chocolate cake.

Supper	2000 hrs. ½ avocado containing chopped lettuce, oil and vinegar dressing. 7 oz turbot baked with garlic, olive oil, fresh lemon juice, 2 boiled potatoes, 1 grilled tomato and boiled broccoli. Coffee mousse with dollop of whipped fresh cream. ½ pint cider. 2 cups instant coffee, each with cream and 2 teaspoonfuls demerara sugar.	2030 hrs. ½ pint lentil and vegetable soup (home-made), small slice of wholemeal bread. Smoked trout cold, tinned petit pois, salad (lettuce, cucumber, tomatoes and carrots). Mince pie (small) with single cream. Coffee mousse. ½ pint cider. Cup of instant coffee and 2 teaspoonfuls white sugar.	1945 hrs. Cheese souffle, 2 roast potatoes, 1 roast parsnip (both roasted in corn oil). Tinned petit pois. Salad (lettuce, tomatoes, green and red peppers, onion and carrots). Coffee mousse with single cream. 1 clementine. 4 oz Muscatel wine, 6 oz mineral water.	2000 hrs. Fish pie, potato slices baked in oil with herbs. Parsley sauce (packet). 2 mince pies with cream. 4 walnuts, 1 water biscuit, blue Cheshire cheese, scrape of butter, 2 sticks of celery. ½ pint mineral water.
Later	2200 hrs. 1 cup of instant coffee, milk and 2 white sugars.	2215 hrs. Mug of ground coffee, cream and 2 white sugars.	2215 hrs. 1 cup of instant coffee with cream and 2 teaspoonfuls of demerara sugar.	2200 hrs. Mug of instant coffee, cream and 2 teaspoonfuls of white sugar.

Notes: mug = nearly ½ pint; cereal weighs about 2½ oz dry.

I remind them to include added salt, chewing-gum, spoonfuls of sugar, sweets, chocolate, cigarettes and all tablets, especially ones bought over the counter. When I talk about a dietary inventory most people only think of foods and drinks, yet they may have been chewing three or four packets of gum every day for years. In fact I once found the blue colouring agent in someone's chewing gum to be the main cause of her symptoms. When she walked into my surgery with a piece in her mouth, I only half jokingly asked her if she had put it on the chart she had been doing for me, and discovered that she had not.

Some people suffer from indigestion, which they have had for so long they do not think it is important. In any case they take antacids from the chemist to keep it under control, so in fact they do not suffer much in the way of symptoms. They keep their indigestion suppressed. In my view, however, both the problem and the tablets are all part of the evidence that needs to be taken into consideration. Moreover, if I were to advise a diet free of cow's milk and the indigestion tablets contained lactose, the condition might not improve. So when patients write out the inventory as fully as possible this is extremely valuable and helps me pick up things I had not thought of.

The other method of completing the four-day inventory is shown in Table 7.2. Here, each item taken into the mouth is listed on the left and the number of times it is taken in the day is indicated with a tick, a dot or some similar hieroglyphic. When you have completed the inventory, sit back and look at it and ask yourself a number of questions about it.

- What do you think of it yourself?
- Do you have too many cups of tea or coffee?
- What is your sugar intake? (Remember a lot is hidden in other foods)
- Do you rely too much on milk and/or wheat products?
- Do you tend to have cheese too often?
- How much salt do you add and how often?
- How much alcohol do you drink?
- Is there anything you tend to consume rather frequently?
- Do you have chocolate in some form most days? (Don't forget drinking chocolate)
- How much 'junk' food do you eat?
- Do you have enough vegetables and fruit?
- Do you perhaps have too much fruit?
- Do you have too much refined flour products such as white bread, pies, pasta, etc?
- Do your foods contain chemical additives such as colourings, preservatives, flavour enhancers, artificial colourings, stabilizers, shelf-life enhancers, anti-oxidants, etc?
- Would you be upset if you were told you ought

to stop having a particular item of food or drink for a month or so? If so, which ones?

- Is there anything about your diet that is odd in any way or that would be considered at all unusual?
- Remembering the general nutritional advice that is recommended and discussed so widely nowadays in the papers and on television and radio, how does your diet stand up?

Can you make any improvements?

Some of the questions, like 'Do you have too many cups of tea or coffee?', are designed to make you look carefully at your diet and ask yourself some honest questions about it. Almost everyone can make some improvements, so why not use this opportunity to do so? Most of the other questions require a 'yes' or 'no' answer, although some of them, like 'How much salt do you add and how often?', require a different sort of answer, which you must consider carefully in case you are addicted to the relevant item.

Although this method is extremely valuable for anyone who is feeling unwell, in helping them to improve their health, it will never do anyone any harm to go through a question-and-answer phase of this sort to see if improvements can be made, even if the person is not feeling particularly unwell. However, in your case the main purpose is to look for addictions and these may be more subtle than you realize, so be as honest as you can.

Charting food preferences

A third way of looking at your diet, or one more sensibly done in conjunction with one of the other inventories, is to compile a chart of your likes and dislikes. Table 7.3 gives a shortened version of what you could complete, but it needs to be expanded to include absolutely everything you put into your mouth.

Patients sometimes tell me that if they have too much coffee, for example, they can develop a headache. This, of course, would go in column A. Any symptom you associate with a food, whether it is taken in small or large amounts, should be ticked in this column. Your body is trying to tell you something which you are ignoring at your peril. Once you have avoided that food deliberately for a number of weeks, usually three or four, having it occasionally after that should do you no harm.

I often find that patients themselves have the information with which to alleviate their symptoms, but they have simply not put the facts together to help themselves. A doctor I met some years ago who asked me to help him with his psoriasis and gout, said that his last bad attack of gout had occurred when he was examining students in the summer. This was in response to questions I asked him about foods he thought might aggravate or cause his symptoms. It transpired that the university

Table 7.2: Food intake over one week

Day	Wed	Thurs	Fri	Sat	Sun	Mon	Tues
Date	6th Nov	7th Nov	8th Nov	9th Nov	10th Nov	11th Nov	12th Nov
Cup of tea	✓✓✓✓	✓✓✓✓✓	✓✓✓✓✓	✓✓✓✓✓✓	✓✓✓✓✓	✓✓✓✓✓	✓✓✓✓✓✓
Cup of coffee	✓✓✓✓	✓✓✓	✓✓✓✓	✓✓✓✓✓	✓✓✓✓✓	✓✓✓	✓✓✓✓
Teaspoonfuls of sugar	✓✓✓✓✓✓	✓✓✓✓✓✓	✓✓✓✓✓	✓✓✓✓✓✓	✓✓✓✓✓✓✓	✓✓✓✓✓✓	✓✓✓✓✓✓
Portions of milk	✓✓✓✓	✓✓✓✓✓	✓✓✓✓✓	✓✓✓✓✓	✓✓✓✓✓	✓✓✓✓✓	✓✓✓✓✓✓
Glass of hot milk	✓	✓	✓	✓	✓		
Chocolate-covered biscuits	✓✓	✓✓	✓✓	✓✓✓	✓✓✓	✓✓	✓✓
Slice of bread (white)	✓✓✓✓	✓✓✓	✓✓✓	✓✓✓✓✓✓	✓✓✓✓✓✓	✓✓✓	✓✓
Butter	✓✓✓✓	✓✓✓	✓✓✓	✓✓✓✓✓✓	✓✓✓✓✓✓	✓✓✓	✓✓
Cake	✓	✓	✓		✓		
Beef				✓			✓
Eggs	✓	✓		✓	✓✓	✓	✓

Whole orange		✓					✓
Orange juice	✓	✓	✓	✓	✓	✓	✓
Cabbage	✓			✓			
Carrots		✓			✓	✓	
Broccoli			✓				
Rice				✓	✓	✓	✓
Potatoes	✓	✓		✓	✓		✓
Added salt	✓✓✓	✓✓✓		✓✓✓	✓✓	✓✓✓	✓✓✓
Bar of chocolate	✓	✓		✓✓	✓✓	✓	✓
Extend this column onto another sheet to include as many foods and drinks as you take during the seven days							

Make a chart like this for yourself. Put the names of each item in the left-hand column, and the day and date at the top of the columns. Put a dot or a tick in the column for each day you have a particular item. In the above example, the patient had five cups of tea and four cups of coffee on Wednesday 6th November, but seven cups of tea and six cups of coffee on the Saturday. Note that she had one teaspoonful of sugar in each cup, and therefore had 75 teaspoonfuls of sugar in the week, let alone the hidden sugar in other parts of her diet. She had at least one bar of chocolate every day – two on the Saturday and Sunday – as well as at least two chocolate-covered biscuits each day. She added salt at most meals.

Table 7.3: Food preferences

	A	B	C	D	E	F	G
Cup of tea						✓	
Cup of coffee						✓	
Sugar					✓		
Milk				✓			
Orange juice				✓			
Orange squash				✓			
Whole orange				✓			
Bread			✓				
Butter			✓				
Cake				✓			
Beef			✓				

	A	B	C	D	E	F	G
Bacon		✓					
Egg			✓				
Potatoes			✓				
Cabbage			✓				
Carrots			✓				
Broccoli		✓					
Rice			✓				
Salt					✓		
Chocolate							✓
Continue the list on							

Key:
A = I dislike it or it gives me some symptoms such as indigestion or headache
B = I am not too fond of it
C = I can take it or leave it
D = I am rather fond of it
E = I am very partial to it
F = I must have it regularly, probably every day, and likely more than once. I would be upset if I was told I must stop having it.
G = I definitely crave it.

had entertained him to dinner the evening before the examination and next day his foot was very painful and inflamed and he had to do his examining in considerable discomfort. He suspected that the double helping of strawberries he had had the night before was the culprit.

When I asked him what jams he had a particular preference for he realized that his wife was particularly good at making strawberry and raspberry jam, to both of which he was quite partial and which he ate regularly. His latest minor attack coincided with the opening of a new batch of jam and he admitted his slight over-indulgence at the weekend before. When he avoided the fruits altogether and then tried them again at a later stage he managed to prove the point very reasonably. More importantly, he had missed the simple obvious connection, despite his own reasonable suspicions, that eating strawberries and strawberry jam might be causing his gout. People simply have to employ a little lateral thinking: their bodies are often trying to tell them something, but they take no notice of these messages.

Once you have identified foods that might be responsible for your problems, especially the addictive ones, cut out all those you have ticked in columns A, G and F. You can always then avoid foods in column E at a later stage. Column D foods should be quite all right, since these are the foods you are particularly fond of without necessarily having any addiction to them.

It will not hurt you to leave out substances to which you think you might be addicted, as you can always put them back into your diet at a later stage if it transpires that these items were quite harmless. I would encourage you to try to put most foods back into your diet in the end anyway. It is never my intention that any food should be avoided totally for the rest of a person's life, unless taking it just once (even after avoiding it for six months or more) makes the person feel unwell. In this case a permanent avoidance of that food is worth serious considera-tion. Some people, for instance, can never, ever eat peanuts again without it threatening their lives. These severe reactions are most unusual, however.

If you are honest with yourself, most of the foods you suspect after going through this list and the questions following it are not likely to be essential to good health, even though they are normally con-sidered healthy foods. For example, while most cheeses are considered good by most nutritionists, with the exception of those like gorgonzola with a high salt content, you will not become nutritionally deficient without them. I accept that this is a controversial issue, but I have no doubt in my mind that this is correct for the vast majority of people.

Having identified your addictive substances, give them up. But first remember you are likely to undergo withdrawal symptoms. So you must plan when you are going to give up these foods and drinks. Don't forget that the effects of withdrawal are likely to last for a few days, but can go on for a week. Fortunately they seldom last longer.

Cross-reactions with tobacco

In Chapter 5 on page 85 I referred to the fact that tobacco, potatoes, tomatoes, aubergines (egg-plant) and peppers are all part of the family of deadly nightshade in the biological classification of plants. Although it does not always happen by any means, many tobacco smokers have a cross-reaction between tobacco and the others. Unfortunately I have no way of telling whether or not you are one of those who do. It may therefore be worth your while temporarily giving up these foods as well, even if they are not among the addictive ones, although I have known one person who was totally addicted to potatoes. Give up these additional foods for at least one month after you have finally stopped smoking. You can then gradually put them back into your diet. If your craving for a cigarette starts to come back or you feel unwell in any way, stop them again immediately and your symptoms should settle once again.

If you give up these or any foods for at least three months, you ought to be able to put them back into your diet on a once-a-week basis without reacting to them. More frequent helpings may make your symptoms come back again, but you will have to do a trial-and-error test on each food. Leaving them out of your diet is only an inconvenience, which should be a fair swap for being symptom-free and feeling well again.

Alkalinizing your body

One further tip that can generally help a variety of problems concerns alkalinization. Whenever a person reacts to a food or a chemical in an allergic type of way, part of the reaction that makes him or her feel unwell is the release of acidic chemicals from a variety of cells in the body. These acidic chemicals make the whole body just a shade too acid for comfort. The more severe the reaction, the more acidic substances are released. The more acid the body is, the more severe the symptoms.

If only one reaction has occurred, but nothing is done to neutralize that activity, the body will gradually cope by excreting a more acid urine over the next few days. After that it will slowly regain its natural balance and the symptoms produced by the imbalance will disappear. If, however, the reaction continues day after day, the body's attempt to excrete a more acid urine will be insufficient to cope with the imbalance, so the body will remain more acid than is good for it.

One effect this acidity has is to retain more nicotine, which tends to be stored in the body's fat cells. If the body can be restored to a more neutral and slightly alkaline state, the fat cells will be encouraged to release the stored nicotine, which can then be excreted through the kidneys. As long as nicotine is stored anywhere in the body it can escape into the bloodstream and create a sense of craving.

To alkalinize the body all you need to do is take small regular doses of pure sodium bicarbonate, obtainable from any chemist. The sort of dose that should do the trick is something like a quarter of a teaspoonful in any amount of water about six or eight times a day.

If you want to be sure you are achieving an alkaline urine, you could ask your chemist for some pH papers, or you might be able to obtain some from your local school's chemistry department. All you need to do is dip a pH paper in a sample of your urine and see if it turns blue. Red signifies acid, alkaline signifies blue. Some forms of pH paper have graded colours, so you will need to know what colour reaction to look for.

Acid pH ranges from 0 to 7, alkaline 7 to 14. The lower the acid number, the more acid it is. The higher the alkaline number, the more alkaline it is. A useful alkaline level to work towards is between 9 and 10.

Too alkaline a reaction suggests you are taking too much sodium bicarbonate, while if it is not alkaline enough you may not be taking sufficient to do the job properly.

Before you start taking the sodium bicarbonate, test your urine for a few days while you are putting your plans in order. Although an occasional test may register slight alkalinity, the majority should be acid, which a non-addicted, non-smoker will produce all the time. Acid urine is normal, as normal metabolism produces acid residues. If your urine shows a persistently alkaline reaction without the addition of sodium bicarbonate to your diet, ask your doctor to have it tested properly for you. There is just the possibility you may have an infection in your urine caused by an uncommon organism called proteus. A proper laboratory test will show whether or not this is present.

To achieve the desired effect, you may need to continue to make your body alkaline by taking regular small doses of sodium bicarbonate for quite some time. How long depends really on how long it takes you to stop wanting to smoke. Ideally you should plan to start taking it when you begin giving up your addictive foods, which in turn should be about a week before you give up smoking.

One or two words of caution. DO NOT take too much sodium bicarbonate if you have ever had heart failure. As sodium bicarbonate contains a good deal of sodium, cut down on your salt (sodium chloride) intake or you may have too high a total sodium load. This could just make your blood pressure rise. It might therefore be a good idea to ask your doctor or the surgery nurse to test your blood pressure before you start taking the sodium bicarbonate and ask to have it checked every two weeks while you take the sodium bicarbonate.

In any case you are unlikely to take the sodium bicarbonate for more than six weeks, and will probably take it for much less. It doesn't taste very nice, but if you put the quarter teaspoonful in a larger volume of water you will dilute the taste sufficiently to make it palatable. It may be possible to get a local chemist to fill some gelatine capsules with the substance for you as an alternative.

The only way you will be able to tell how long you should continue to take sodium bicarbonate is to judge how you feel. If the whole plan works well for you, then you should be able to stop taking it sooner rather than later. You may have to restart for a short while if craving returns, but only trial and error will tell you how long to continue.

8

Stop smoking slowly

The preliminaries are over; you now have to stop smoking. I will be describing three different methods. The first, detailed in this chapter, is gentle and easy. In the next chapter I will describe a much harsher method, but one that may appeal to some people. The third method, set out in Chapter 10, is a more unusual one and is based on the practice of ecology clinics, although it can be self-administered. Read them all and then choose for yourself.

Preparatory arrangements

The first thing to do is to decide the day you intend to start giving up smoking. Prepare yourself by putting notices all over the house and anywhere you frequent in order to remind yourself when you are starting. Put notices on the dining-room table, the fridge door, the toilet seat, the bathroom door, the walls of all corridors in the house where you may turn a corner and come across the reminder. Don't forget your car, or both of them if you have two cars, your office, any sports locker you use, perhaps the garage door. I once read an interesting article that described how the world's No 1 women's tennis player at the time, Martina Navratilova, felt she was not playing quite as well as she ought to and her friend Billie-Jean King realized that Navratilova was not concentrating on the ball every time she hit it. Tennis balls were then put everywhere in her house so that wherever she went she had to look at a tennis ball – so it almost became a subconscious act. You need to do something similar. Even a world-class tennis player needed some sort of reminder to help her concentrate and there is no reason why you should be any different.

Don't be anxious. You have read this book, you know what you are going to do and you should be excited at the prospect of a time in the near future when you will no longer be a slave to the weed. It is true you may have to go through some degree of withdrawal symptoms, but you know what they are about, why they may occur and what to do to minimize them.

It can be a good idea to give up with someone else. Your spouse or partner might not be a good choice, but a friend who has wanted to give up for a long time could be helpful. You can ring each other to give each other support. Try to minimize any adverse effects that you may be suffering from and encourage your friend to do the same. Concentrate on how well you are coping: 'It's not as bad as I thought it would be'. Be positive. Know you have made a wise decision. Be determined not to give in this time. Be confident you will never smoke again.

Plan a routine. Consider a form of exercise. If you are a regular sports player, plan extra activities. If you are unaccustomed to exercise, appreciate that you are going to become fitter as a result of giving up smoking and think of an activity that appeals to you. Perhaps you should take up walking. Drive to local beauty spots you have been meaning to go to for years, get out of the car and walk around. Use the wonderful views and paths as a positive approach to all things good around you and to try to take your mind off any discomfort in your body.

I am not expecting you to give up smoking on Day 1. Indeed it may be unwise even to try. Some people do try to do this and find their withdrawal symptoms go on, and on, and on. The symptoms do eventually go, but giving up abruptly like this can make you suffer quite badly (as do those around you!) for an unnecessarily long time. Following some of the advice I have given in this book should help to make things easier.

In fact I want you to smoke on Day 1 and then go on to reduce both the number of cigarettes and the amount of each cigarette you smoke. But first let me suggest one more way to keep in mind the fact that you are now actively doing something about giving up smoking.

Put into your hand the container from which you normally take a cigarette, the container that you carry around with you. Is it a special cigarette case given to you by a member of your family or a friend, or was it a business or retirement present? Or do you always take a cigarette out of a pack that you bought from a tobacconist? Whichever it is, you must do something about it. You have already put up notices everywhere you can think of as a reminder to yourself that you are giving up smoking, but you may just happen to walk out of the house with a pack in your pocket and simply light up without thinking what you are doing. Habits die hard.

I suggest you wrap a piece of white paper around the pack and write on it something like: 'Think – do I need to smoke?' in bold red letters, so that you cannot possibly take a cigarette out of the pack without seeing the reminder. As an alternative, to prevent you just flipping the lid open without looking at the pack, and especially if your 'pack' is a favourite cigarette case, wrap whatever it is in a plastic bag, together with a warning note. You cannot possibly take a cigarette out now without a reminder, through touch and sound, to make you at least look at the pack. You must then see the warning note.

Concentrate on each cigarette

It is now Day 1, the day when you are going to start giving up smoking. You have already made your preliminary arrangements and you are about to smoke your first cigarette of the day. Before you take the cigarette out of the pack ask yourself a few simple questions:

Do I really need to smoke yet?
Can I leave it a bit longer?
How do I really feel?
Is it that bad at present?
Have I the will-power to last a little longer without smoking?

These questions will help to reinforce the fact that you are making a positive effort to give up smoking. No system is going to help you at all if you do not make some effort yourself – the main stimulus to giving up smoking has to come from you, for no-one else can do it for you.

Your decision to light up a cigarette on this first day need not be too stressful. If you can put up with the withdrawal symptoms a little longer, do so, but *do not let yourself suffer*. What one person can tolerate another cannot. Besides, it depends upon you, the circumstances in which you have chosen to start giving up smoking and a whole host of factors in your life I cannot possibly anticipate here.

Remember one thing, many smokers say they will give up when they are ready. But they are never truly ready, because they think smoking is helping them in a stressful situation. In fact, all that each cigarette is helping to relieve is the withdrawal symptoms from the last cigarette they smoked and it is this feeling that they classify as 'stressful'. While life may be stressful for them, the degree to which they suffer from that stress is made far worse by these withdrawal symptoms. A vicious circle has been set up. The only way to break that circle is to make a determined effort to do something.

Do not wait until you are suffering. Somewhere along the line on Day 1 you must accept that withdrawal symptoms are beginning to bother you. Many people will not find the feeling too bad, it will be more a sense of missing something, feeling unable to get on with life or simply being fidgety. Your blood nicotine level has fallen below the craving line (see Figure 6.1).

If in doubt, don't be anxious. Simply take a cigarette out of the pack, light it and inhale the smoke *gently*. Don't suck it deep into your lungs, merely inhale – *once only* – as you have always done. After 30 seconds (time it), ask yourself the following questions:

How do I feel?
Have any of those withdrawal symptoms lessened?

Do I feel better?
Have I come up above the craving line?

If the answer to any or all of these questions is 'Yes, but not enough to settle me,' inhale again. When another 30 seconds have passed (always time this with the second-hand on your watch or a clock), ask yourself the same questions. After the second, third or possibly the fourth inhalation, you may well be comfortable enough to feel you have relieved the withdrawal symptoms. You must now be above the craving line. If this is the case, stub the cigarette out in a large ashtray and notice how little of the cigarette you have smoked and how much you have discarded. Note down how many puffs it needed to reach this stage. Preen yourself that you have already won battle No 1. You have consciously smoked less.

Set about normal daily living. Try to forget all about smoking and withdrawal symptoms. After all, they are no longer affecting you. What has happened is that your blood nicotine level has come up above that arbitrary line, the craving line, some-where below which your craving for a cigarette and withdrawal symptoms begin. As I have already explained in Chapter 6, all you need to do is bring the level above that line and your symptoms will disappear.

If your blood nicotine level is not raised above

that line, your withdrawal symptoms will remain. More importantly, if you bring yourself *too far* above the line, the rate-of-change effect may come into play; your cravings will develop more quickly and be more severe the further above that line you go, as they will have further to fall.

If you get yourself *only just* above the craving line (enough to clear the symptoms), the fall in blood nicotine after that will be so gentle that the onset of craving symptoms will be equally gentle. It is fair to say that the lower below the craving line you go, the greater the withdrawal symptoms you will subsequently experience (as hypoglycaemic symptoms can develop if your blood sugar falls too low). However, those symptoms are only likely to come back strongly if the *rate of fall* is rapid, which it should not be if you don't let your blood nicotine level go too high in the first place. The way to prevent this is by not smoking the whole of a cigarette, but merely enough to lift you just above the craving line. (See Figure 8.1.)

Having found the smallest number of inhalations of your first cigarette that lifted you just above the craving line and cleared your symptoms, you now get on with whatever you were doing and wait and see what happens. If you judged it correctly the first time, your blood nicotine level should fall slowly and the level at which the craving begins again should be lower than it was the last time. In effect

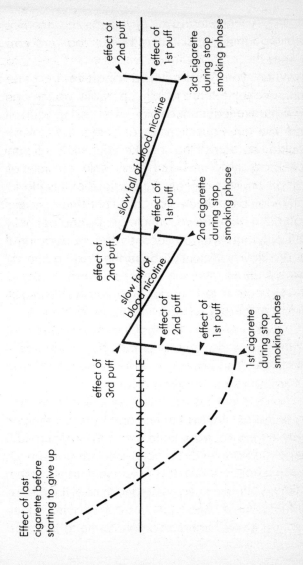

Fig. 8.1: The effect on levels of blood nicotine when starting the Stop Smoking campaign

this means that the height of the craving line has been set lower than it was before that previous cigarette.

When your desire for a cigarette becomes strong enough for you to light up again, go through the whole procedure once more, first asking yourself again the same questions as on pages 139–140. If possible, do something to take your mind off any developing symptoms, but don't hold out for too long, otherwise it defeats the purpose of this plan.

Remember, when you do light that second cigarette, make sure you inhale gently and normally *once only* and wait 30 seconds before deciding if you are now sufficiently above the craving line for your symptoms to subside. You must make a conscious effort to consider how you feel and you must give yourself enough time to think about it.

I hope you will notice that the gap between the first and second cigarette is already wider than it used to be. You have now won the second battle. You are no longer smoking as often.

Don't forget to stub the cigarette out into the very same ashtray as the first and don't let anyone empty it. Stub each cigarette out so that it cannot be reused. I want you to keep seeing how much tobacco you are wasting. The sight of so much wastage will reinforce your intention of giving up, as you realize how much money is in that ashtray. You might just as well hand a £5 note to the tobacconist and ask to watch it being burned or thrown away.

Keep up the same procedure for the first day or two. Make a note each time of how many inhalations you need to bring yourself above the craving line. Slowly that craving line will sink. When it touches bottom you will no longer have any cravings or withdrawal symptoms to cope with. When it stays rock bottom you will have finally kicked the smoking habit.

The rate at which the craving line sinks will vary from person to person, but in any case it should not take too long to do so. Keep taking the small doses of sodium bicarbonate regularly to help your body eliminate all nicotine (see page 133). The cravings and potential withdrawal symptoms will go when your body is finally free of all nicotine.

This clearance of nicotine from your fat stores is important in the long run because, as your blood nicotine levels fall, your fat cells release some of their stored nicotine in order to maintain a balance in your bloodstream. If you smoke, however, your blood nicotine level will be higher than the level in your fat stores, so that more nicotine will be deposited there.

If you do not replenish your blood nicotine level with your usual intake of cigarette smoke, the level will nonetheless rise to some extent, as your fat stores liberate nicotine to bring the level up. This makes you crave a cigarette. Over the months, you can slowly eliminate all nicotine from your body. When it has all finally gone, your craving to smoke disappears.

Other tips

This process of purging yourself of nicotine can be speeded up by using sodium bicarbonate to alkalinize your body, but it does not seem to raise your blood nicotine level enough to interfere with the plan to give up smoking. Alkalinization will help your fat cells to release the stored nicotine, but more importantly it will also help your body to eliminate it via your kidneys. A further reason why sodium bicarbonate helps is because too much acidity generally can be one cause of people feeling ill after any 'reaction'. Alkali neutralizes the acid and makes you feel better.

For reasons that are not clear, long before you have totally cleared all nicotine from your body your craving line will have sunk so low that you lose all the symptoms of craving. This point will be reached rapidly in some people, more slowly in others. I have no idea why this difference occurs.

Similarly, some people can give up addictive substances with consummate ease and not suffer at all. I have known a 90-cigarette a day man give up without a murmur. Likewise a man whose arthritic hip was caused by drinking tea made from 80 tea bags a day, stopped drinking tea without going through any withdrawal symptoms at all. On the other hand, some people give up their two to three cups of tea and coffee a day and suffer badly for a few days.

Cigarette smoking causes more long-term reactions in the body than food reactions, because of the way nicotine is stored in the body. If a smoker gives up without reducing smoking gradually in the way I have described, or without using one of the methods detailed in the next two chapters, cravings do seem to go on for longer. Simply giving up and suffering fails far too often. If you use the method as explained in this chapter, your cravings will disappear fairly early on even though your body may not have eliminated all its stores of nicotine.

There is an interesting further step you can employ which might help, although I do not fully understand why it does. It is a slightly different approach, but can be just as effective, and should be tried only after you have managed to apply the general method of increasing the interval between cigarettes and smoking enough to bring your blood nicotine level just above the craving line.

You don't see it so often nowadays, but in the past I can clearly remember watching a man have a few puffs of a cigarette, stub it out very carefully on the sole of his shoe or a wall, blow on it to make sure it was completely out and then carefully tuck it behind his ear and leave it there until he fancied a few more puffs, when he would relight it.

Once you have established a pattern of smoking the odd puff (you must stub out and destroy every unused length of cigarette and never try to reuse it), the next time you feel a need to smoke, take a cigarette out of its pack and place it in the gap between your ear and your temple (where a carpenter might keep a pencil). Start a stop-watch or check the second-hand of your watch and count 60 to 90 seconds, after which time take the cigarette and put it back into the packet without smoking it.

For reasons that are not clear, the presence of a cigarette in the electromagnetic layer around your body has some effect upon the levels of nicotine within your body, or at least an effect similar to that which nicotine has on your body. Leaving a cigarette in close proximity to your skin for between a minute and a minute and a half can often reduce your craving to smoke it, but this works better if you have already started to reduce the frequency between, and the total amount smoked of, each cigarette.

As before, you must concentrate. When 60 seconds have passed, in fact even as that time is approaching, consider seriously how you feel. If you feel better, but believe there is room for improvement, leave the cigarette by your ear for another 15 to 30 seconds. After a total of 90 seconds, there is no further benefit from leaving the cigarette there and you might as well put it back into its box. It won't hurt to leave it behind your ear, but the more actions you perform as reminders that you are actively giving up smoking, the better.

If the effect of putting the cigarette behind your ear is to make you feel better and not need to smoke, then you have won battle No 3. You have been able to avoid smoking a cigarette that you took out of its packet to smoke. If putting the cigarette by your ear doesn't help in any way, you may now proceed to have enough puffs of that cigarette to bring you above the craving line, as you have been doing all along.

Sooner or later, it is to be hoped sooner rather than later, you will quite simply not want to smoke again. The craving line will have reached the bottom. Once you have reached this stage, destroy all unused cigarettes by crushing them into the same ashtray you have been filling up all along and not emptying.

This method requires you to think of what you are doing, to concentrate on a particular pro-gramme and to assess regularly how you are feeling. You still have to push yourself each time. Every time you consider smoking, you must try to last a little longer without a cigarette and when you do smoke, you must consider after each puff whether or not you have come above the craving line. You must be honest and you must do this *every* time. You must try to avoid going any further above the craving line than you can avoid. You are trying to lower the craving line all the time.

One question I cannot answer is how long it will take for *you* to kick the smoking habit. The range is a few days to about four weeks. Even if it takes you the longer time, the symptoms of craving rapidly diminish as the system starts to work. You simply seem to reach a plateau where you may feel you are stuck and are not able to get any further. You may be down to two puffs per cigarette, at four cigarettes a day, but any less than that and the craving becomes unacceptable.

What is happening is that nicotine is being liberated from your fat stores and keeping your blood nicotine level temporarily high enough to stop the craving line from permanently hitting bottom. It clearly does touch bottom some of the time, but if you find yourself under pressure more acidity may be formed, which you may misread as a withdrawal symptom. Any level of blood nicotine at all seems to have more of an effect if your acidity is raised. So it may help to take a few more doses of sodium bicarbonate.

Some people have found that sodium bicarbonate is sufficient to clear symptoms of craving at a certain stage; certainly if you seem to have reached a plateau this is worth a try. However, I don't think it is worth doing this on its own if you are still smoking normally and then try to give up completely.

Obviously I don't know how large your nicotine fat stores are, or how long you have been smoking. In theory it might be imagined that the fatter you are and the longer you have been smoking, the greater the problem is and the longer it will take to clear your body totally of nicotine. In fact it just isn't like that. It depends upon other aspects of addiction in your system. The more addicted you have been, not only to cigarettes but also to items like coffee, sugar, cheese or whatever, and the worse your diet has been in general terms, the more problems you are likely to have. If you have been abusing your body in many ways for a long time, it will have developed a higher level of acidity and so it is likely to have deposited that much more nicotine.

I would like to say it is as simple as that, but it isn't. When I have taken a complete medical history from some people, I have feared that they would not only suffer bad withdrawal symptoms, but would also struggle to stop smoking and would probably take a long time to achieve it. While my clinical experience has been correct most of the time, I am pleased to say that people have broken the rules often enough for me to hope that you too will get away with minimal symptoms.

Positive attitudes and your immune system

Despite the considerable time I spend with all my patients, during which I explain everything I can to them, I still don't have enough time to understand people's every personal problem, all the stresses they may be under, or to get to know their personalities well enough. I have the impression that the real successes are in people who are determined to succeed, so that attitude of mind somehow depresses the craving line or helps to make the body more alkaline – probably a combination of the two. No doubt other factors are involved as well.

For instance, we have hardly mentioned the immune system at all, but I am aware from my own studies that smoking can depress the immune system. So can stress and a deficiency of vitamins and minerals. However, a positive attitude can somehow work wonders on some people's immune systems, which may be a relevant factor.

To take an analogy, I have worked for a number of years with a local cancer self-help group. We encourage people to do all sorts of things, but primarily to take charge of their own getting better. We advise them and show them what they can do for themselves. We teach them how to relax, meditate and visualize. We advise them to eat a healthy diet, based upon our own researches. We tell them what they *can* do to help themselves and explain how they can get themselves better.

Right from the beginning I develop a strong sense about those who will make it and those who will not. Those who really want to do something for themselves get better. But far too many want everything done for them and don't want to help themselves. This is the sorry state our health service has brought us to. We let the doctor do all our thinking for us. The doctor treats us; we let him or her treat us. It doesn't involve us doing anything apart from turning up for an appointment and submitting to whatever treatment is prescribed, or trying to remember to swallow some tablets three times daily.

While this approach will at least relieve the symptoms of many people, surely it is better to try to find the underlying cause and remove it, letting our bodies heal themselves. But this means we have to be involved. If we take control we lighten the load on our immune system. The only way a regular doctor may be able to help here is to give you such a heavy dose of a tranquillizer that you are in a permanent zombie-like state and effectively quite relaxed. This approach might calm your immune system, but it won't let you enjoy life at all.

Some years ago a study was carried out in an Australian hospital. When people left a particular set of wards where a close relative had just died, they were asked if they would be willing to submit to a blood sample being taken for some research. The test showed that all people in a state of shock at bereavement had clear evidence of suppression of their immune systems. The rate at which they recovered from the shock was mirrored by the recovery of their immune system. Those who had not got over the bereavement after a number of months not only showed continuing immune-system problems, but were also now showing signs of additional forms of ill-health.

Anything that upsets your immune system is potentially harmful. My own studies show that cigarette-smoking can suppress the immune system, while equally the correct nutritional, environmental and psychological approach can support the immune system and bring it back to health. This will have an overall knock-on effect to make a person feel better. I also feel sure that an improved immune system will more effectively help the smoker's craving line to reach bottom and stay firmly there.

I remember meeting Dr Hugh Cox from High Wycombe for the first time in the mid-1970s, when we had both been invited to talk at a meeting at Charing Cross Hospital in London. Dr Cox was describing his experiences with helping people to give up smoking through the use of acupuncture. He claimed a success rate of about 75 per cent. During question time, a number of experienced acupuncturists asked him how he achieved such a high rate, when all properly carried out studies had only shown 50 per cent success. I remember Dr Cox's reply. He said, 'I look my patients in the eye and firmly say to them: "This time you *will* give up smoking"'. I am sure that this is what achieved the extra 25 per cent success rate.

Science at present is far too strict. It assumes that if you do something correctly, the scientific way, then it has been proven beyond doubt that that method works. This is a head-in-the-academic-clouds approach. I wouldn't doubt for one minute the value of what are called scientific methods. Unfortunately, however, far too many doctors believe that theirs is the only way. They forget that their primary job is to get people better. In their headlong flight for scientific excellence they seem to forget the importance of the patient.

Not so long ago I read a newspaper article which was somewhat critical of a medical colleague who practises in a similar way to me. It described the methods used in the clinic and showed in what way they were not only different, but controversial, even though it also quoted many grateful patients. The most extraordinary part of the whole piece was the quotations from at least two orthodox specialists, who to all intents and purposes said that any doctor could get patients better if he or she admitted them to hospital for a few days and did a number of things to them, in particular fussed over them. Countless thousands of people who read the article must have wondered why orthodox medicine doesn't do that all the time if that is all that is required to get someone better.

I don't deny the value of a caring, understanding approach, but I firmly believe there are plenty of excellent doctors who have tried their utmost to help their patients, yet who have totally failed far too often for their own liking.

Full explanations, of the sort I have given here about how to give up smoking, relax people and so give their immune systems a boost. It is far more distressing not knowing what your symptoms signify and worrying about whether or not you have cancer, or some other so-called incurable disease like multiple sclerosis. I know no-one wants to be told bad news, but once the bad news has been given to you, you can stop worrying about what the diagnosis might be and start doing something about it. The knowledge of the bad news alone can bring a remarkable sense of relief.

The psychological approach to ill-health is taken into account far too seldom. The psychological problems of smoking withdrawal symptoms, or the *fear* that they will occur, are played down. My hope is that after you have read this book you will understand all that is going on and this will not only encourage you to try to give up smoking, but will also take away the agony of possible withdrawal symptoms. As I have said, there is no need to 'suffer' from withdrawal symptoms. There are many ways of limiting or abolishing them, but the first is to hope and believe that they will not be nearly as bad as you have been told they will be.

9
Stop smoking through revulsion

This method is clearly not for everyone, but it is interesting to read. You may recall the laboratory technician I described in Chapter 5, in whom we found smoking had a disastrous effect upon her blood sugar, what we did and what happened. It might be worthwhile reading pages 95–100 again, just to remind yourself. It was my observations of this patient that gave me the idea I am now going to describe.

Ex-smokers who wish they weren't

The principle of this method is based on the idea that when some people give up smoking on their own without anything but will-power, they remember the day, date, time and hour when they smoked their last cigarette. They yearn for those heady days when they were happily smoking whenever they wanted to. No-one was nagging them to give up. All their friends were smoking too and no-one realized that smoking was potentially harmful to the health of smokers and of those around them. Life was tranquil.

Now the anti-smoking lobby has made smokers the minority. It has made them pariahs in the midst of their erstwhile friends and colleagues. No longer is it possible to smoke wherever and whenever a person wants to. Smokers have to go into special areas designated for them. In some places of work those who are still smokers are the odd ones out, instead of the majority.

A few have succeeded in giving up without any difficulty. They make life miserable for those still smoking, as they suggest that giving up was easy. To make matters worse, they tend to be ardent anti-smokers. They seem to be reformed characters. They no longer seem to want to be with people they once considered as friends if the latter are still smoking. Indeed, these ex-smokers seem to find other people's cigarette smoke to be even more annoying and aggravating than is reasonable. They persistently avoid a cigarette smoker as much as possible and tend to be the ones who object out loud if a person smokes near them. If someone smokes in a no-smoking area, they are the ones who point it out.

My point is that many people who did eventually give up smoking remember their smoking days and their last cigarette with pleasure. They don't seem to be able to let go. Somehow they must be retaining a form of craving, even though they must surely have lost all their body stores of nicotine over the months since they last smoked.

I think that their problem may no longer have anything to do with nicotine levels or the effect of nicotine on the body. It is more that they retain in their memories an image of what they still consider was a pleasurable experience – the casual cigarette with a cup of coffee after a meal, the relaxing cigarette when the pressure was on, the mid-morning cigarette to take stock of things.

Because this memory is so potent for some people, it is unfortunate if someone who is contemplating giving up smoking happens to meet a person who is still hankering after free-smoking days, even if that person has not smoked for some time. Sheer will-power probably got these ex-smokers there in the end, but they might well retain such a strong memory of those pleasurable days that they can convey a sense of doom to those who want to give up. They describe how much trouble they had when they gave up smoking and the extent to which their families and friends suffered from their withdrawal symptoms.

Such people are all doom and gloom, probably no longer craving a cigarette, but still not over the sense of cigarette deprivation. If they did succumb, they might find it quite distasteful, but they dare not try as they believe it will start them smoking all over again.

The problem with these people is that they remember smoking *with pleasure*.

What this method of helping a person to give up smoking is all about is making the memory of cigarettes an unpleasant one. This is brought about by over-smoking.

Preparatory arrangements

Like the gentle method, this harsher method needs planning. Read this chapter through thoroughly and satisfy yourself that this way is for you. It doesn't suit everyone. Indeed, I would say it is only suitable for a small percentage of people who want to give up. The gentler method is far simpler and makes more sense scientifically.

The method requires that you choose a day when you are to stop smoking completely. I have found that, if you are going to embark on this course but otherwise continue your normal daily life, the first day of your working week, usually a Monday, should be Day 1. If you are going to do it and take one or two weeks' holiday, then it doesn't matter when you start.

Warn everyone around you that next Monday is Day 1 when you are going to stop smoking, although you are only stopping for five days in the first instance. Tell your colleagues at work, not so much as to get their sympathy or encouragement, but mainly so that if you are slightly irritable everyone will know why. You might perhaps have a colleague who would like to give up in the same way at the same time as you, although it would be sensible for them to get a copy of this book first, read it through and decide which method to try. I am sure the gentler method is best for most people and apart from that there is plenty of information worth reading first before anyone gives up smoking.

Put notices everywhere for Monday morning saying 'NO SMOKING'. Before you leave for the weekend on Friday evening, make sure you have put a sign on your desk at work as a reminder. When you wake up on that Monday morning, it must be clear from signs all round you that you are starting today. Stay off cigarettes for FIVE DAYS. Do your best to avoid others who smoke, so you must identify those people and places in the run-up to Day 1. This may need to be planned carefully.

Getting through the five days

Do not go anywhere near a tobacconist. You must have already cleared your house, pockets, car, office and anywhere else you can think of, of all cigarettes. If you go to a restaurant, sit in the no smoking area and start convincing yourself that you are a non-smoker, or certainly soon will be. If there are any smokers there, don't look furtively or longingly at them. Even better, choose a restaurant that doesn't allow smoking at all.

Start conning yourself. Don't be afraid to use good old-fashioned psychology on yourself. If you are feeling miserable or suffering from withdrawal symptoms, tell yourself you know why they are occurring and try to minimize the effect they are having on you. Remind yourself that you are making a positive effort to give up smoking completely and that you are doing something that will improve your health in the long run.

If you have a family, reason with yourself that giving up smoking should help you to live longer, will help prevent you from getting cancer, will stop polluting their bodies too, and that you will be around longer to enjoy them all. Do something to occupy yourself and take your mind off any symptoms that might develop.

Remind yourself that if you are craving something, you have let that something take over your body and your life and you have only yourself to blame for that.

Several people I have seen as patients who complain of any number of symptoms, especially headaches, have suffered withdrawal symptoms when I have altered their diets. In some people, stopping caffeine and/or tannin can produce a most devastating headache for a number of days. Some have come back a month after the first visit so 'impressed' by their withdrawal symptoms that they are totally convinced of the value of the lesson. They feel that if avoiding something can produce such severe withdrawal symptoms it has to be something they must stop taking and try to avoid for the rest of their lives.

So treat any withdrawal symptoms you have as nature's warning sign. Fortunately, symptoms of withdrawal from anything can be overcome, although, to be fair, it can be very hard on some people. But time is a great healer and the majority of ex-smokers fortunately only need a short time.

Day 6

For Day 6 you need a 'friend' who is also a bit of a sadist. You will need to have primed someone, who should ideally have read this book, to understand what to do and, more importantly, why. The more informed the friend is, the more completely he or she will co-operate and do what I suggest. This friend can, of course, be your spouse, partner, parent or sibling, but someone from outside the family circle is probably better.

On Day 6, which is likely to be a Saturday for most people, pick up your helper or arrange for him (or her) to come to your house early in the morning. Go with him to the nearest tobacconist and buy a packet of 20 cigarettes of your favourite brand, or ask him to buy a pack on the way over to your house. You must not, however, have bought the cigarettes the night before and started thinking about them. DO NOT SMOKE YET, but wait until you arrive home.

Once at home, light up your first cigarette. Instead of sitting there inhaling gently and suavely, suck the smoke deliberately and forcefully deep into your lungs. Be more positive about your inhaling than you have ever been before.

Before you have had time to consider the effect of the first puff, put the cigarette to your lips and suck on it again, once more sucking the smoke in deeply. Before you have had a chance to think how you feel, inhale again. Inhale persistently, deeply and completely, and finish the whole cigarette. Whereas you might well have taken ten minutes to smoke a casual cigarette in the past, you should now take half that time.

During the two days or so before Day 1, when you started giving up for five days, you should have collected the stubs of your regular cigarettes, put them in a jar with a tight lid on it and handed this to your friend. On Day 6, when you start to smoke again, your friend should tip the contents of this jar into a large ashtray, so that you start with it fairly full.

Before you stub out your first cigarette on Day 6 into the nearly full ashtray, light cigarette No 2 with No 1 and deeply inhale all of the second cigarette.

Take as short a time to inhale the whole cigarette as you did with cigarette No 1. Before you stub out the second cigarette (into the same ashtray), light your third cigarette with it and go through the same process.

Light your fourth cigarette with the third cigarette, your fifth with the fourth, the tenth with the ninth, the twentieth with the nineteenth. Inhale the smoke from each cigarette deep into your lungs. Make it hurt. Your friend the sadist must keep insisting that you go on smoking. There is a chance that the very first cigarette may make you feel quite ill, but you must persevere. Your helper is there to make sure you complete the job, is there to make sure you feel really ill. If you vomit, so much the better. The more ill you feel the better the effect upon you, but you must be pushed to extreme limits. The purpose of this method is to make your memory of your last cigarette a really awful one. You must have firmly imprinted upon your memory just how disgusting that last cigarette was, how terribly ill you felt.

Your helper may feel you have learned your lesson before you reach cigarette No 20. He must be aware, however, that you might be putting on a bit of an act and are not suffering all that badly. If in doubt, he must urge you to smoke another cigarette.

When he is convinced that you truly are feeling ill, that your lungs are really hurting and that you have learned a very good lesson, he should put a little whisky into the ashtray you have now filled up and get you to put your nose close to it to smell the disgusting smell coming from it. Have you ever wondered why the smell of cigarettes in pubs is more pungent and potent than anywhere else? The reason is that tobacco and tobacco smoke dissolve more effectively in alcohol and, of course, the air in pubs contains droplets of alcohol.

When you take a nose-full of the ashtray full of stubbed-out ends dissolved in whisky (just describing it makes me feel sick), be aware that it may make you not only feel sick, but actually vomit, so either be near a toilet or have a bowl ready for such an eventuality. If you are physically sick, the impression on your memory will be all the stronger. Personally, I hope you are sick. This whole process is designed to be so awful that you never want ever to smoke again. No doubt you can see why.

Not suitable for everyone

I have described this method to give you a choice. I have put people through it, but not many. Most find the gentler method more appealing and it also makes sense to them. If my limited numbers trying it are representative of the effect it would have on larger numbers, then something like 60 per cent will find it works first time, 20 per cent actually try it once more, or even twice, while perhaps 20 per cent might find it doesn't work for them.

Some people must *not* use this method. Anyone who has cancer, especially of the lungs, or any lung disease such as emphysema, bronchitis or asthma, should NOT try this method. It may also be inadvisable for anyone with a poor heart to attempt it, but otherwise I cannot think of any other reason why a person ought not to do it. If in any doubt, you must consult your doctor.

I am sure you can appreciate that the many inhalations of cigarette smoke deep into your lungs would act as a great irritant and could clearly exacerbate bronchitis or any of these conditions. As cancer of the lung is probably caused by smoking in the first place, smoking *more* would clearly be inadvisable, as it might make the lung cancer worse. (Quite honestly, I would be horrified if anyone with lung cancer was still smoking. Surely someone must have helped such a person to stop smoking already.)

How does it work?

The gentler method of giving up smoking has a certain ring of scientific truth about it. If this is valid, then trying the harsher method doesn't really make sense if it works. Smoking up to 20 cigarettes all at one sitting should effectively make your blood nicotine level high and hence deposit more nicotine in your fat cells. In due course this nicotine has to leach out into your blood, to be eliminated slowly. Why then do so many people find that it does not produce a craving?

Could it be that the psychological effect of the horror induced by this harsh method pushes the craving line down low, so that you cannot crave because the craving line has effectively reached rock bottom? Alternatively, perhaps the psychological effects somehow interfere with the craving centre – assuming there is one – and suppress it sufficiently to prevent the craving from occurring. I don't know what the explanation is. I only know that it works.

If you read and consider the third method of giving up, described in Chapter 10, you will realize that some of my explanations do not fit all the observations. This does not mean that they are not valid, but simply that an alternative explanation is not always appropriate.

One final – and most important – point about the five-day method is that if it puts you off smoking, for a week or more anyway, and the need for a cigarette then returns, it would be sheer disaster to have 'just one more cigarette'. This would start the smoking habit off all over again.

If, after having given up successfully this way, albeit temporarily, you fancy a cigarette, you have two choices. First, suffer a bit but let the symptoms fade so that your memory still retains the horrors of the last cigarette. Your alternative is to try the method again. The second time will make you ill far more quickly and the system will reinforce your memory.

Protect yourself with vitamins

One of the reasons why cigarette smoking causes ill-health is because of the formation of what are called free radicals. These toxic substances damage tissues if they are not dealt with, although in one form they protect the body. Free radicals are inactivated and rendered harmless by anti-oxidants such as Vitamins A, C and E.

Circulating white blood cells are part of the body's defence mechanism. They use free radicals to kill germs by means of what is known as the 'oxygen burst'. The bacteria and viruses are engulfed and exposed to a high concentration of oxygen within the cell, mainly through the production of hydrogen peroxide. During this time, oxygen free radicals are inevitably formed, which could theoretically damage the white blood cells themselves. The cells are protected, however, by carrying within themselves enough anti-oxidants to cope with any free radicals that might form. The cells die and are therefore of no help to the body's immune system if their stocks of anti-oxidants are insufficient.

The more cigarettes a person smokes, the more anti-oxidants they need. One reason why some people develop lung cancer from smoking, while others do not, could be to do with their diet and hence their nutritional state. Most smokers damage their tissues over the years, damage that might be prevented by taking many more vitamins and minerals – although clearly it would be best not to smoke in the first place.

If you try this heavy chain-smoking method, please first prime yourself with anti-oxidants, starting at least a week before you begin. I would suggest you take the following:

Vitamin A, 10,000 IU per day
Vitamin C, 1g three times per day
Vitamin E, 400 IU twice daily
Any strong multivitamin/multimineral tablet two or three times daily

Be aware that Vitamin C can cause stomach upset in some people, but with any luck it will not affect you. In case it does, start with 1g once a day for two or three days, move to 1g twice daily for another two or three days, then, if still OK, increase to 1g three times daily. You can easily obtain 1g tablets from most local health-food shops and chemists, while your local pharmacist will stock the effervescent 1g tablet you drop into water. It wouldn't do you any harm to try a quarter tablet (250 mg) once a day to begin with and gradually increase the dose, but the fizzy forms are more expensive once you have reached 1g three times a day.

If you have not had a particularly good diet for many years and you have also been smoking for a long time, you could sensibly take the above quantities of these vitamins for many months. After that it is worth considering a gradual reduction until you are simply taking the multivitamin/multimineral tablet once a day or every so often. However I cannot advise you much in this area as I do not know what your personal needs are. You might therefore be wise to seek the advice of a practitioner trained in nutritional requirements. Sadly, your own doctor has probably not learned enough about this to be of help to you and in fact might well dismiss the whole idea.

10

Stop smoking through neutralization

This third method of giving up smoking owes its existence to the original clinical ecologists who devised neutralizing techniques. People like Dr Ted Randolph of Chicago (who celebrated his eightieth birthday in 1991) and Dr Joseph B Miller of Mobile, Alabama, are those who come to mind. However, the person who first introduced me to this type of medical understanding and management of all forms of ill-health was Dr Richard Mackarness, a psychiatrist at Park Prewett Hospital in Basingstoke, Hampshire, who has now retired to Australia. It is mainly to him, through a book he wrote on this subject, that the information in this chapter should be credited. Having tried it on patients, I know it can work.

There is one problem I have in describing this method. Having given you meticulous details about how craving occurs and how hypoglycaemia may be involved, following that by a very common-sense approach to giving up smoking, this method breaks all the rules – well, certainly all the rules I can think of. But, to be fair, so does the second method I described in Chapter 9, the one where you give up for five days and then chain-smoke.

Still, it does not matter. So long as this way works, I do not mind. In the end, if it catches on sufficiently, scientific explanations will follow sooner or later. Most steps forward in medical care start with an observation which is found to work in practice, but may take years to be subsequently proven by scientific validation.

This method involves finding a dilution of cigarette smoke dissolved in water (or some suitable liquid) that will actually turn off a person's craving. But first, as with the other methods, some background information is worthwhile to help you understand it.

General applications of the technique

The principle involved here is called neutralization and it is basically a system that can be used to test a person's sensitivities or allergies to foods, drinks, inhalants (like dust, house-dust mites, fur, pollens and so on) and chemicals (such as gas, petrol and diesel fumes, perfumes and the like). It can also be used to de-sensitize them, in other words to alter the body's immune system so that the person no longer reacts to that substance. If you have been found to react to a food, neutralization should allow you to eat that food without being made ill.

Each food, drink, chemical or inhalant needs to be tested, one at a time, for which reason the process can be time-consuming if many allergies are suspected. Experienced clinical ecologists know how to cut corners, possibly by only testing for those substances identified by asking questions of the patient.

Let us take a simple example of a person who gets a skin rash from eating strawberries, which he or she would like to be able to eat without becoming itchy. As another example, we could think of an asthmatic who is allergic to house-dust mites.

The preparation of strawberry or house-dust mite is made by dissolving a fixed weight of the substance in a fixed volume of liquid, usually 0.9 per cent NaCl (sodium chloride), more simply known as isotonic saline. That means its strength is balanced with blood serum. This basic mixture is called the concentrate and those who use the system came to an agreement about how to make this concentrate starting-point so that everyone is following the same method.

A fixed volume of concentrate, say 10ml, is then put into a second container and 40ml of saline is added, making a one in five mixture. This first dilution is called No 1. Then 10ml of No1 is diluted with 40ml of saline to make dilution No 2, and so on as far as you want to go. Most clinical ecologists tend to have dilutions available down to about No 10 in case they need them, but in fact they do not often need to use dilutions that go down so far.

The patient is then tested in one of two ways; sometimes the two are mixed. One method is to put a drop of the dilution under the person's tongue, the other is to administer an intradermal injection (into the superificial layer of the skin). Whichever method is used, a reaction of some sort is expected. If the skin is injected, a weal may be produced. If a drop is put under the tongue, the patient may develop symptoms.

The ideal end result is when a sublingual drop does not produce any symptoms (or clears any that have been produced by an earlier dilution of greater strength), or the skin weal produced by injecting the substance into the skin disappears in 10 minutes. There are various rules that have to be learnt and followed, but the principle is as I have described it.

Clinical treatment of smokers

In terms of giving up smoking, the symptoms of craving can be 'turned off' by finding a suitable dose, or 'end point', that does the trick. The person who wishes to give up smoking must attend a clinic in a state of craving to smoke, otherwise the method does not work nearly as well and it may be impossible to find the correct end point. Alternatively the wrong end point may be supplied, which is no help to the patient, although it is unlikely to make things worse.

So the patient arrives at the clinic craving a cigarette. The No 2 dilution is injected into the skin of the upper outer part of the arm (there is no point in starting with No 1 as that is very rarely the end point). After about 10 minutes the patient's skin reaction is checked and he or she is asked how they feel. Usually there is a positive weal on the skin, but a lessening of the craving.

Dilution No 3 is then injected and a further 10 minutes allowed to elapse before a judgement is made on whether or not the end point has been reached. Further intradermal injections are made at 10-minute intervals, each time the response being gauged until the weal is considered to be negative and the cigarette craving has gone.

Having identified the patient's dose, a bottle of drops of that dilution is prepared and the patient is instructed to put one drop under his or her tongue whenever symptoms of craving develop. Some people recommend doing this anyway once every hour for the first few days, gradually lengthening the gap between doses. Most, however, simply need to carry the drops with them wherever they go, to use whenever the symptoms of craving develop.

As the drops do not contain a preservative, it is best to keep them in a fridge if possible. That way they should last longer. However, with any luck the need for a cigarette will have cleared within a matter of days, so making the drops last longer is irrelevant.

Treating yourself

How can you apply this method to yourself? Before you give up smoking using this method, measure out into a glass an amount of water that is easy for you to repeat – say three tablespoonfuls, so that the glass is less than half full. Light a cigarette and exhale slowly through a straw, bubbling your exhaled cigarette smoke through the water. One cigarette may be enough to make a fully saturated solution, but you can use two or three if you like. You must, however, write down what you did, how much water you used and how many cigarettes you puffed into the water so that you can repeat the process later if need be. Call this your concentrate. Make dilutions No 1, 2 and 3 from this. You can always make more dilutions later if you need them.

Try to obtain from a local chemist a few eye- or ear-dropper bottles and put just one drop of the first dilution under your tongue and see how you feel in about 10 minutes. If you feel less of a sense of craving, feel worse, or do not feel any better, try a drop of No 2 and go through the same procedure again.

If you do not notice any obvious effect from any dose down to about No 6, go back to No 1, but this time try three drops. You should not throw away your dilutions until you have completed the test. If three drops of any dilution turns off your craving, that is your 'dose' and you must put three drops under your tongue each time from then on. It is possible you may have to go back to dilution No 1 and try five drops. If that does not work, you can try more, but it is unlikely the method will work for you this time.

Because of its simplicity, if the test did not work first time it is worth trying again a few days later. It may even then if it did not earlier. I do not know why. It may simply be that your system is more sensitive and receptive at certain times.

Once you have chosen your treatment dilution, decide for yourself whether to put the drops under your tongue only *when* you crave, or, if you are a more regulated person, to do it at fixed intervals. Personally, I think the best method is to use the drops only when you crave a cigarette. When you worked out your original dose, you found from experience how well it got rid of your craving. So each time you want a cigarette now you know it will work again.

This approach to giving up smoking is rather akin to homoeopathy, although the dilutions used here are not nearly so great. Exactly how homoeopathy or this method work are not yet known, but the giving of a dilute dose is like the 'hair of the dog' effect the morning after a heavy drinking session the night before. The symptoms of the let-down, the craving symptoms, can be relieved by smaller doses of the same substance, which is why you make the dilutions. For the best effect, you have to find the specific dilution that does the job perfectly for you. Once you have found it, it seldom changes as long as you use it regularly. On rare occasions the correct dilution needs to be reassessed, but if you have thrown your original dilutions away, please ask someone else to make your concentrate for you. If you were to do it yourself after not having smoked for a while, you could undo all the good you have done so far.

Reinforcing the method

Presumably this method effectively pushes the craving line so low that in due course (seldom more than two to three weeks, after which cravings disappear) you no longer need the drops at all. At this stage, call yourself a non-smoker. This is important. Preen yourself that you have successfully given up smoking. Be proud of what you have achieved. Think positively about how much better you are going to feel. Start a programme of exercises, if you do not

already do them, to improve your heart and circula-
tion. Start to unclog your arteries. Be determined that
you are going to improve your health and become
as fit as possible in order to help you live healthier
and longer.

As cigarette smoking uses up Vitamin C, I would
strongly advise you to take about 1g three times
daily with meals for at least a month, then perhaps
1g twice daily for a month and then 1g per day. One
gramme is probably a useful dose for most people
to take on a daily basis, but if you do keep this up,
don't let it become a fetish. Get into the habit of
taking it, but do not worry in the slightest if you forget
it.

Whether or not you need to take any sodium
bicarbonate to alkalinize your body in order to help
clear your body of nicotine if you use this method is
debatable. Provided the craving line falls so low that
you no longer crave a cigarette, it may not be
necessary to do this. On the other hand, if you were
to start taking a more alkaline diet this would not
only be generally more healthy, but would also
probably be sufficient to leach nicotine slowly out
through your kidneys and so get rid of it totally over
a matter of weeks. Until all the nicotine has been
cleared from your body, there is always a slight risk
of a desire to smoke again. By now a minor craving
of this sort should be easily resisted. You know it was
a good thing to have given up, so a simple 'good

talking to' by yourself and occupying your mind in some way should do the trick. If you still have the original concentrate in your fridge (which it is wise to keep for a few months just in case), you can always make a few dilutions and use the system again.

One thing is of great importance. NEVER, EVER, SMOKE A CIGARETTE AGAIN.

11

Prepare yourself to stop smoking

Having read this book thus far, you should have a clear idea as to why you ought to give up cigarettes and why it need not be too much of a problem. Even if you do suffer from withdrawal symptoms, you should now understand them and be all the more able to cope with them. Let us, therefore, summarize how to proceed.

I assume you will be choosing the gentler method, although I don't want to tell you which way is best for you. It is up to you. Whichever approach you decide upon read that chapter again, Chapter 8 for the gentler method, Chapter 9 for the harsher method, Chapter 10 for the neutralization technique.

Planning to stop smoking slowly

Set a day and date when you are to start. Having made up your mind to give up smoking, and having read this book through to the end, you must decide when to stop. There is no point in putting it off. So when is it sensible to start?

Check your diary and try to avoid starting when you are busy. You need a reasonably calm time, if such a time exists for you. It is probably best to be at home rather than travelling away from home, otherwise it will be difficult to concentrate. In particular you need those reminder notices. It is not so easy in a hotel or someone else's office.

Which day of the week to start depends on your lifestyle. If you go out to work, a Saturday is probably the best day to begin, provided of course that you don't go to work on that day and the next. Two days at home to concentrate and get things off to a good start are very useful. By Day 3, you should have yourself properly organized. You might even have already stopped smoking.

The day before you start needs the preparation of those reminder notices. Discuss with someone you live with where to put them. Involve as many other people in the home as is reasonable. If you are the only smoker, they will all want to help, especially children. Let them design the notices. That way it will be fun, particularly if they can put some cartoons or other drawings on them. It might be something they can do for you at school. If they do some special designs for you in Art class, it might stimulate other children to encourage their parents to give up in the same way.

If you have any especially interesting or amusing incident while you are giving up, write to me, or perhaps let the newspapers know. The more publicity there is, particularly if it is humorous, the more other smokers might be willing to try to stop. I think everyone agrees that smoking is no good and indeed positively harmful to your health, so everything that can help other smokers to give up is important.

Before you start, it might help to try to obtain some pH paper from the local chemist or school chemistry department. Test your urine for a few days so that you get the hang of it. Obtain supplies of pure sodium bicarbonate to take once you have started to give up smoking. There is no real value in taking sodium bicarbonate before Day 1.

Did you go through your diet to look for potentially addictive foods? Have you already given up such items and do you feel better for it, even if you did have a few days of withdrawal symptoms? If you haven't already done so, don't forget to start giving them up on Day 1. There is no reason why withdrawal symptoms should be any worse for giving up more than one addictive substance at the same time. The only problem may be that you crave more than one thing. Which to have – a cigarette, a bar of chocolate, a hunk of cheese, a cup of sweet tea or coffee? All must be resisted. You are determined that Day 1 will be your Victory Day.

During the evening before Day 1, don't go out and get drunk! It would be silly to wake up the next morning feeling hungover. You certainly wouldn't feel like giving up that day, apart from which you wouldn't be in the right frame of mind to concentrate on what you were doing.

Start Day 1 in a relaxed mood. Wait until you have some degree of *need* for a cigarette before you light your first one. Delay the first cigarette of the day for as long as possible, without suffering. Remember that most smokers smoke out of habit, half the time not really needing a cigarette. When the time comes to light the first one, inhale it normally, but be totally conscious of what you are doing and why you are doing it. Observe how you feel and when you feel better. Please, stub the cigarette out *as soon as* you have had sufficient nicotine. Follow the full plan until you no longer need to smoke any more.

It is perfectly all right for you to start taking vitamins and minerals before Day 1. Any cigarette smoker requires extra anti-oxidant vitamins, so these can be started at any time. As you probably have quite a lot of catching up to do, you can go on taking the vitamins I advised on page 171 for at least three months after you stop smoking, too.

As any tablet you take, which includes essential nutrients like vitamins and minerals, can – if rarely – upset your stomach or produce some sort of side-effect, it might be sensible to begin the vitamin and mineral regime some time before you embark on this method of stopping smoking, in order to make sure it suits you.

One thing that some smokers fear when giving up is putting on weight. This is because, if they don't know what they are doing and what is going on, when they stop smoking some people start nibbling or sucking sweets, anything to take the withdrawal symptoms away. They are so accustomed to doing things with their hands and mouth (lighting a cigarette) every so often, that their mouth feels neglected, so they keep it busy.

If, however, you follow my plan, there will be no need to nibble out of sympathy for yourself. What you do eat should be *good* foods, as you will already have decided to eliminate from your diet those that you are addicted to, which are nearly always the ones that would make you put on weight all too easily.

In any case, if you control your withdrawal symptoms by following my plan those symptoms should be minimal and hence there should be no need to nibble all day long. So, if you are not going to put on weight, your reason for not giving up smoking has been eliminated. You therefore have no reasons left for not starting to give up straight away.

Planning to stop smoking through revulsion

The harder, harsher method of giving up needs its own degree of planning. Remember you are going to give up *totally* for five days and will not have the gentler method available to let you down slowly or to control your withdrawal symptoms. However, there is no need to fear them. They may never occur. You may simply miss your smoking, but feel some sort of reinforcement is needed. Plan when Day 1 is to be. Prepare your No Smoking signs. Inform everyone what you are about to do – 'inform' rather than 'warn' because the latter would assume that you will have bad withdrawal symptoms, ie that you are already expecting the worst. Try to be positive. I have known some people give up for five days and find it quite easy, but actually build up such an anxiety state about how horrible they expect to feel when they do chain-smoke on Day 6 that the very thought has had the desired effect. None of them actually followed the complete plan: they never smoked again because the very thought frightened them sufficiently.

Make sure there are no cigarettes anywhere in the house, your car or your office, etc. Select the person who is going to push you to the limit on Day 6. Remember to collect all your cigarette stubs for a few days before Day 1, so that your ashtray will already be full when you smoke your 20 cigarettes on Day 6. Don't forget to have some whisky to put into the filled ashtray when you have smoked enough.

Obtain some vitamins and minerals as described on page 171. You can start taking these whenever you want to. Sodium bicarbonate is also obtainable from your local chemist.

When you have completed this harsher method of giving up smoking, be hopeful that you will never smoke again. Remember that the main intention of this method is to make your memory of smoking a very painful experience. You must never, ever, smoke again with pleasure.

If in a week's time you fancy a cigarette, you must not smoke just one cigarette. You must buy a whole packet and chain-smoke all over again until it really hurts. You may need the help of a friend again.

Planning to stop smoking through neutralization

If you decide to treat yourself in this way, first obtain some eye- or ear-drop bottles from a chemist so that you can make your dilution in them. Remember that you must be in a state of craving when you test the dilutions and that you may need a little patience to find the dilution, or end point, that will work for you and turn off your craving. But the method is simple to follow.

As with the other two approaches, it is a good idea to take vitamins, especially Vitamin C, to counteract the effects of cigarette smoke in your body. Taking sodium bicarbonate may be useful in clearing your body of nicotine, though following an alkaline diet is likely to be more helpful.

Your attitude is also of vital importance. Regard yourself as a non-smoker from the moment you start taking your dilution. Tell yourself – and mean it – that cigarettes are no longer controlling you and that you will never smoke again.

You have read this book. You have chosen which method to try. You know what to do. Now get on with it – and the best of luck!

Index